# The Write Stuff

*A guide to effective writing in social care and related services*

Graham Hopkins

Russell House Publishing

for Jo Hopkins
she knows why

*First published in 1998 by*

Russell House Publishing Limited
4 St. George's House
Uplyme Road Business Park
Lyme Regis
Dorset
DT7 3LS

© Graham Hopkins

**British Library Cataloguing-in-Publication Data:**
A catalogue record for this book is available from the British Library.

ISBN: 1-898924-41-4

Printed by Bookcraft, Midsomer Norton
Typeset by TW Typesetting, Plymouth, Devon

# Contents

# Acknowledgements

---

*'Pray know that when a man begins writing a book he never gives over. The evil with which he is beset is as inveterate as drinking – as exciting as gambling.'*

Anthony Trollope

Me? I'll check out the boards, take the price and then get a round in. Second time around, I'm still not too sure about how to write an acknowledgements page or what to say. However, my publishers assure me that nobody ever reads them (except those being acknowledged, I guess). So, already feeling tailed off, we're under starters orders with the prospect of this going all the way to the wire.

As we sort ourselves out and pass the mile marker, I'd like to thank all those who galloped their way through the heavy going of the drafts spotting (binocular-like) with all their usual glee my tie pin mist aches. And who, more important, made valuable tips on the book's (that is, my) style, purpose and stance. They who are *all those* are (the draw being no advantage): Kes, Jo Hopkins, Frances Rostron, Eric Davis, Marcus Woolley and Julie Cann (and who did, this time). Thanks to you all. Especially as you all suggested silkier alternative phrases or sentences which now wear my colours and shamelessly parade as all my own work. We're passing the two marker, now.

Least but not last, fat bazza thanks to Kathryn Stone for doing all those agent-y things, putting up with the mood swings, and for believing. Thanks (again, but out of the top drawer this time) to Marcus who provided the graphics for the *using visuals* section in Chapter 8: *Layout*, and who co-wrote the text around it. Thanks also to Geoffrey Mann and Martin Jones at Russell House for their support, understanding and for backing me.

And lost but not leased, once again, final thanks to Stephen Hicks, who is, without question, the best illustrator working today: in my book, anyway.

Well it's been nip and tuck all the way to the line, but we've flashed past the post and I'm going to leave that one to the judge. I have to hold my hand up and say I had hoped to win hands down. Here's the finishing line: I'm told that publishing is a form of legalised gambling; well, the hare's running at Romford and the lad's broke again.

**Graham Hopkins**
September 1998

# Preface

*The Write Stuff* is a good practice guide, for people working in social care and related services, that shows you how to plan, research, structure, write and edit your written work. Drawing on practical examples, it will help you to write more effective letters, memos and reports that get the results you want.

Its companion volume, *Plain English for Social Services*, also written by Graham Hopkins, aims to introduce and promote the principles of plain English. If we are to communicate well with people, we must make sure that our writing is clear, easy to understand and user friendly.

This acclaimed book refreshingly blows away the cobwebs of stodgy and bloated writing that tends to characterise social care, and helps you to get to grips with writing in simple, plain English. As with *The Write Stuff*, the style of *Plain English for Social Services* is defiantly informal and highly readable – its serious message being delivered in an entertainingly informative way.

The book draws on actual examples of public writing produced by 26 social services departments in England and Wales and six social work departments in Scotland. *Plain English for Social Services* shows you how to write concisely, express yourself clearly, shorten your sentences, avoid jargon and gobbledygook, and how to write in a more human way. It also relishes its task of exploding writing myths (you **can** start a sentence with *And* if you want), and seeks to improve our understanding (thus reducing our fear) of grammar and punctuation.

Writing is a skill, not just something that we should be expected to know how to do well. *Plain English for Social Services* and *The Write Stuff* will help you to do it better.

# Introduction

# Chapter 1 – Introduction

*'Writing is easy; all you do is sit staring at a blank sheet of paper until the drops of blood form on your forehead'*

Gene Fowler

**writing**

Writing's easy, isn't it? Nothing to it. A doddle. A pushover. A piece of cake. Plain sailing.

*'Let's face it, writing is hell'*
*William Styron*

Do you know anyone who thinks this is so? If so, then please ask them to move among us mere mortals and share with us their secret. Because I believe that most of the population here on planet down-to-earth who when confronted with an empty page, experience their collies wobbling and sense their spine shivering (in an upwards and downwards motion).

I believe that everybody has a fear of writing. It's a fear that is more obvious to some than others, but it's there, all the same, in even the most confident writers. On training courses I have asked people to explain out loud what a *keyworker system* is. They have all told me and everybody else in the room what it is. When I then ask them to write down what they've just told me, they delay, they re-think, they write, cross out and re-write. In a word, they *struggle*.

I think this has a lot to do with the permanency of writing. Say something and it's gone. Write it down and it's with us forever: it's hanging around at the back of our careers awaiting for the best (that is, worst) time to come back and haunt us. Or, more immediately subject us to the potentially humiliating judgement of others. So we think (at least) twice before writing anything.

*'I love being a writer. What I can't stand is the paperwork'*
*Peter de Vries*

Also when we commit words to a life sentence on paper we worry that we might not come across as distinguished enough. We feel the need to convince our reader that we know what we're talking about. So, how do we sound distinguished? By using pompous words, of course. This will prove to the poor reader just how rich we are in knowledge, reputation and importance. So, with no-one daring to tell us otherwise, we continue to trade in bloated writing.

## writing badly or what?

All this fear, worry and concern leads us to writing badly. And this doesn't necessarily mean using bad punctuation, grammar or spelling – although these are important, and are indicators for a lot of people against which to judge the quality of writing. For me, even writing that can't be faulted for punctuation, grammar and spelling can still be examples of poor writing. Writing is all about communicating. I think that if your intended audience understands what you're saying – and at the first time of asking – then that is good writing. As simple as that. The second you fail to communicate, then that is third rate writing of the first order.

Other reasons why our writing can at times fail to communicate can, in some cases, be traced back your 'education, education, education' (*Blair, T, 1997*) at your school, school, school. I blame the teachers, me. Or, at least those who teach English. The emphasis is to teach creative writing and ensure an appreciation of English literature at the expense of teaching writing as a means of everyday communication. Most of the official writing we do in the real world once school's out (*Cooper, A, 1972*) amounts to letters to bank managers (and their ilk) and letters of complaint – neither of which are necessarily unrelated. And the writing required by our jobs.

'Whereas "good" English used to be defined as a special, high-flown and rather artificial style thought to be suitable for public occasions, official correspondence and the like, it is now felt to lie in a more natural tone of voice'
*B A Phythian*

And what training have we? A (drilled in) understanding that Ted Hughes used animals to make poetic comment on man's apathy, or something. Very useful when writing a letter of complaint:

> *My overdraft has laid dormant as a caged tiger but now I, heartened by the short sharp stench of purchasing, need to shock the beast to vitality and strut my negative balance. Hope – is there any?*

We carry around with us vague recollections of advice (i before t but not after supper, or something) that disserve us well. We were told time and time again not to use the same word twice in the same sentence. In our essay writing we were encouraged to show a wide vocabulary – so we think that bigger words are better, when in reality easy ones often come out on top.

The class of 97 Labour government's (and in my view, misguided) obsession with attainment has meant that schoolwork is aimed at passing tests, exams and key stage assessments. In all of these, we are writing for people who know the answers. So we write the answers in the most impressive way possible. We seem to be pushed towards sounding impressive and being expressive. All our words are stretching to hold the moon when a simple down-to-earth grasp of the real world would do the trick.

**the writer as reader**

A good exercise to rid yourself of flabby and out-of-shape writing is to think of yourself as a reader first, and a writer second. Think of the things that would attract you to, say, reading a report. If you made a list it might include some or all of the following:

- *the subject (clear title)*
- *attractive layout and design*
- *headings and clear sections*
- *summary*
- *short and precise*
- *attention grabbing cover page*
- *glossary*
- *contents page*
- *easy to read*
- *easy to look at*

Now ask yourself: how often do you write reports that fit this bill? This is the first step towards putting yourself in the reader's shoes. Your job as an effective writer is to make things as easy as possible for your reader. The job of *The Write Stuff* is to help make things easier for you.

**how the book works**

*The Write Stuff* has been designed to take you through the logical stages of writing a letter, memo or report. We begin by looking at planning your written work, and in separate detailed chapters, look at how to organise, structure, layout and edit your work. We also examine your writing style and word choice, and look at how and where you write.

We make use of real examples from social and health care to help illustrate the points being made. Also, to help put the theory into practice, we have created a case example. We follow the process of writing a report – on customer care – from receiving the brief to the completed report. This helps us to see how a report evolves.

**team writing**

*The Write Stuff* presumes that when you write at work you are mostly left to your own devices. Many organisations find team writing effective. If team writing works for you – good. An underlying principle of *The Write Stuff* is to encourage you to find out what works best for you. While the principles of writing effectively will also help effective team-writing, this book is aimed mainly at those who write on their own.

**writing in social care**

In social care and related fields, we spend a lot of our time writing. From letters to memos, calling in at reports, and back again, we seem to be spending longer and longer at desks, at keyboards and on laptops (although the less said about the latter, the better).

And yet what training is available on writing? We would not let a social worker work with a client unless we were confident that the worker was well trained and knew what they were doing. So, why should we let someone loose with a pen or sit them in front of a screen and just let them get on with it? But we do. Writing is something that we're all expected to know how to do. Some things do come naturally to some people (singing voices, acting talents, Coventry City's ability to give away soft goals) but writing ain't one of them, mate.

'The most essential gift for a good writer is a built-in, shock-proof shit detector'
*Ernest Hemingway*

Writing is not easy; it's a skill, a craft. But as with all crafts it can be taught, learnt, practised and improved. And then practised more and improved further. *The Write Stuff* is designed to teach you the basics of effective writing. It's text book stuff, all right: but it aims to teach with a smile on its page.

# Planning

# Chapter 2 – Planning

*'Grasp the subject, the words will follow'*
Cato the Elder (234–149 BC)

---

**summary**

*What you need to know before you start writing*

*There are three questions to answer:*

- **why are you writing it?** – knowing what your objective is, having a clear brief, and clear timescales

- **what do you want to achieve?** – how this influences the form, content and tone of your work

- **who are you writing for?** – understanding your target audience, writing for a variety of target audiences, choosing a main target audience, the influence of those senior to you

**introduction**

Throughout the pressure-cookered, business-oriented, bottom-lining 1990s service demands seemingly increased in alarming contrast to decreasing resources. In response, many organisations fell under a managerial mania for things like *quality* and *planning* as means to providing more for less. But rather than explain how simple these things are and how they should simply be part of your everyday work, two virtual industries were born.

*Head of Planning* or *Head of Quality* became titles worthy of Assistant Directors. Planning and quality became special stand-alone services. With the distressingly inevitable arrival of new buzzwords and jargon, the hijacking of the ordinary for the

*'In preparing for battle I have always found that plans are useless, but planning is indispensable'*
*Dwight D Eisenhower*

special was complete. To those who spoke the language, planning and quality were essential, integral and strategic. To everyone else they were remote, confusing and the root of that most popular of questions about those who planned or quality-ed: 'what *do* they do?'

I provide this somewhat over-simplistic, one-sided analysis of planning (with a sprinkling of quality – to taste) for no other good reason than to convince you that while planning is, indeed, a very important task, it is, nonetheless, a very simple idea. And probably not what you have been bamboozled into imagining it is through a barrage of managementspeak.

If you're going on a journey to somewhere you've not been before, you might check out a map and work out the best route; or, if you're like me, you check times, frequency and pray for the *existence* of public transport. That's planning. Will you have something to eat before you go, on route or when you get there? That's planning, too. Do the people you may be travelling with have any ideas, suggestions or requirements? Taking time before you start to work out what's best – that's planning, that is. There's no doubt that the better you plan a journey, the easier, more comfortable and better it will be. Writing is no different.

You need to plan the route your message will take, choosing carefully the words that will take you to your destination – *your conclusion* – in the simplest, most efficient and effective way. This chapter will look at ways of helping you to do this.

The amount of planning required will depend on the written piece of work you have to do. A short memo, for example, acknowledging a meeting and confirming your attendance will take little planning; whereas a report on, say, an annual review of a service will clearly take considerable planning. We're going to look at some general principles but you will need to identify the ones relevant to your piece of work.

## before you write

There are three questions you should always ask yourself before you write a word. These are:

- *why are you writing it?*
- *what do you want to achieve?*
- *who are you writing for?*

**why are you writing it**

*Why?* is the greatest question in the history of the world ever. A stock question for children and an often irritating one as it's usually the hardest one to answer. (But only if you discount the

*Where?* question when related to your manager, obviously). There's a scene in Oliver Stone's film *JFK*, where the investigator Jim Garrison, who is investigating the assassination of President John F Kennedy, asks a retired CIA agent: 'He was a danger to the establishment – is that *why*?' The agent responded: 'That's a real question, isn't it? The *how* and *who* is just scenery to the public: Oswald, Ruby, Cuba, the Mafia – keeps 'em guessing like some kind of parlour game; prevents them from asking the most important question – *why*?' It certainly is a question to be fired at everything you do – whether you're sat behind your desk, cowering in a book depository or standing on a grassy knoll.

I've often thought that if you can't answer satisfactorily **why** you are doing something, then perhaps you shouldn't be doing it; particularly if your only answer is related to the *'we've always done it this way'* family. So, with writing (or *scripting* in the current managementspeak) we should ask ourselves *why* we are writing it; what is the purpose? The precision, detail and clarity of your answer to this question depends entirely on your brief.

## make sure your brief is clear

Put simply, the clearer the brief the clearer the work. If you're replying to a letter or memo, your brief is usually straightforward. You should address each point raised (and usually in the order raised by your correspondent as that's the order that the points are important to them). However, if you're being asked to originate a piece of work, you will need a clear brief – the more detailed the better.

Quite often the reason you are writing something is because you've been asked (that is, *told*) to. If a senior manager asks (that is, *tells*) you to 'put together something on that new bit of legislation for a committee report next week', your instantly developed selective hearing selects to ignore the alarm bells and you accept the challenge. You pull up your socks, roll up your sleeves and generally readjust or realign any other dissenting item of clothing or part thereof. And you do this why? Because you're a team player; because you want to get on; because you want to prove your worth. This is an all too understandable and sadly recognisable, but potentially disastrous situation. The minute you sit down in front of screen or A4 pad, all the team playing, getting on, worth-proving inspiration is lost. Suddenly, you find yourself adrift up a well known creek with only a pen for a paddle. And your pen leaks.

And so it begins. Questions slap you in the face: what legislation? What about it? Is the report an information piece or something that will require decisions? What about the implications for other services? What should be our position on the issues? What other information do you need to know about? How long should the report be? And so it continues.

**if your brief is unclear**

If you are unclear about *why* you're writing something this will be reflected in *what* you write: it will be unclear, muddled and directionless. Your message and arguments will come across as even more bewildering than your Director's dress sense.

If getting a clear brief proves difficult, then draw up your own brief and submit that for approval. As *The Write Stuff* will repeat to irritation: it is your job as a writer to make life easy for the reader. And a good brief makes your job easier. So, don't leave home without one.

**timescales**

Your brief should clearly tell you how long you have to complete the work or, in managementspeak, the *maximisational timeframe for project delivery*. As with money and people, time is a resource and needs to be budgeted and well managed. If a report is required quickly this will limit, for example, your research time or your chance to produce drafts.

You should also check the requirements within your organisation. For example, procedures for reporting, authorisation, guidelines, house style, any restrictions on circulation and so on.

**what do you want to achieve?**

You need to be clear about what your intended outcome should be; what is it you want to happen as a result of your letter, memo or report? How do you want your audience to react?

**what are the possible outcomes?**

There are five possible reasons for writing in social care and related services. These are:

- *to inform*
- *to find out*
- *to persuade*
- *to enforce*
- *to record*

**to inform**

Working in public service a lot of our time is spent, formally and informally, providing information. Sometimes this is asked for (*can you send me a list of registered childminders?*), and sometimes this is provided as a matter of course (*information leaflets on available services and so on*).

Within your own and partner organisations you may write memos and reports to inform colleagues and decision makers about issues that are about to come up or things that are already happening.

**to find out**

We write to find out information. This might be a letter to someone asking for clarification or for information on how they deal with a particular issue.

A consultation document may be sent out to find out what people think about certain issues. For example, what should be considered in a community care plan? A draft report might be sent out to find out what people think about how you have researched, handled and written your report. These people will usually be those whose opinion you trust, who are expert in the area covered, or who may have taken part in the preparation of the work.

**to persuade**

This may take the form of an internal memo trying to persuade people to be part of **another** working party of a sub-group of a task force of a committee set up by an advisory body. You will need finely tuned powers of persuasion to convince them that *this* working party *this* time has some real work to do, that it *will* have a real influence on policy and that it *will* be effective. Honest.

A report requiring a decision may be an exercise in persuasion. For example, a request for a budget increase. If a particular issue has, say, four options that you detail objectively, without preference – this would allow the reader to make their own mind up. However, and much more likely, if you clearly favour one option, it is your task to persuade the reader to agree with you. This might mean playing up the negative sides of the other options. Or ignoring all other options in favour of the wholesome, 95% fat free, righteous, clean, proper option – the only one open to all decent, law-abiding, god-fearing, animal-lovers the world over.

If the response favours your choice, then you've done a good job in persuasion. If the report has mixed reactions or more information is called for, then it might be that you haven't argued your case well enough or your readers have detected a bias that has raised their suspicions.

**to enforce**

In order to protect vulnerable people, and having had, depending on the circumstances, perhaps failed to effect a change in attitude, care or services, you may need to resort to enforcement. For example, if a registered care home was found to be providing care or services that put residents at risk, then the registering authority can take legal action which may result ultimately in the closure of the home. They may also be able to issue a notice of intent – a warning to improve things to a specified standard within a set timescale or else legal action will be taken.

See chapter 5 *Writing style*

Naturally this type of letter or notice would be formal in style, tone and content. It is something that could be used in court or at a tribunal and needs to reflect the seriousness of the situation.

**to record**

Recording appears to upset a lot of people. They feel that social care has become obsessed with records and paperwork. However, recording **is** essential. Records are proof that something did or did not happen. If you don't record a visit in a case file or record what you bought (with receipt) for a resident in a home from their personal allowances, you don't have proof that any of these things happened. In health, for example, clinical notes represent a legal document which are ultimately the responsibility of the Secretary of State for Health.

A memo or letter that 'confirms' what was verbally agreed with someone becomes a record of that conversation or agreement. The minutes of a meeting or supervision are all records. Filling in forms, questionnaires and assessments are all records.

ISO 9002 is the European-ised version of the British Standards Institute quality standard BS5750. If you encounter ISO 0992, apart from battling through skirmishes with a complicated and vague language that betrays its military origins, you will discover that records are at its heart. The standard requires you to say what it is you do, requires you to do it, and then requires you to prove it. And to prove it you need records. You may later realise that after a long and expensive campaign to be awarded ISO 9002, the spoils of war are somewhat limited. The award, for example, is certainly no guarantee that you provide a quality service. And anyway you should be wary of anything that uses the initials ISO to stand for the International Organisation for Standardisation. I wonder what the IOS 9002 is like.

Records are a form of insurance. Records are evidence, should you need it, that you acted with what your legal section might term 'due diligence'. An American lawyer even went so far as to say that a memo is not there to inform but to cover your back. Sad times. But true.

## who are you writing for?

### *target audience*

While it is important to know the objective and the intended outcome of what you're writing, both of these will count for nothing if you don't take into account **who** it is you're writing for. You need to put yourself in their place/situation/position/ stead/shoes (*delete as applicable*). It's usually worth spending some time thinking about the things you would look for if you were the person receiving it.

### *one-to-one*

acronyms are words made out of the initials of titles, such as DIAL: *Disablement Information and Advice Line*

If you are writing a memo or letter which is basically one-to-one it should be easier to understand and picture your reader. For example, if it's a colleague then you will be able to use acronyms, abbreviations and jargon used regularly within your organisation. However, if it's a letter to a member of the public who is enquiring or complaining about a service then that type of shorthand would be inappropriate. So, it's important to:

- know your reader
- understand what they know
- understand what they *need* to know
- decide the best way to tell them.

### *variety of audiences*

You will soon confront more difficulties when your piece of work has a potential variety of audiences. For example, an inspection report on a residential care home or a nursing home could be read by:

- the residents or patients
- relatives, friends or representatives of someone living in the home
- the manager of the home
- the staff of the home
- owners of the home
- senior managers
- people responsible for purchasing places at the home
- elected members or members of the health authority executive
- people who are interested for themselves or for a member of their family moving into a home
- other inspectors
- any member of the public (now that all reports are open to the public).

Under the Registered Homes Act 1984, health authorities have the responsibility for inspecting nursing homes, and local authorities have the responsibility for inspecting residential care homes.

It's a dilemma to know how to write something that meets the needs of such a wide audience. Health authority inspectors have been required since 1 April 1998 to make their inspection reports open to the public. This requirement had been enforced on local authorities since 1995. Previously, in many cases, health authority inspection reports were simply letters from the inspector (representing the registration authority) to the owner. The target audience was clear and defined. Now, amid some indignation, they are considering the implications of their reports being open to the wider public – as in *'wider the public have access to our reports?'*

## deciding on your main target audience

This dilemma has been approached by some inspection units by deciding on who their *main* target audience is. The local authority I worked for consulted with all interested parties and asked: *who should the main target audience be*? The overwhelming response was 'the public'. So, we redesigned the layout of reports so that they were clear, simple but sharp; developed a house style, which included writing in plain English; and packaged our reports attractively – even producing reports with full colour covers to help them stand out on library shelves.

It also meant that if an inspector talked about, for example, a *'keyworker system'* – this was explained. Homeowners and staff did not feel patronised at having these things spelt out either. This was because they understood that the report was written for the public who might not understand the day-to-day terminology of a care home. However, the reports we produced tended to be rather long. And no matter how simple the language, a 45 page report is simply not user-friendly. So we also produced a four page (a folded A3 sheet) summary report. This gave the highlights of the report, listed the facilities available at the inspected service and informed the reader where to get a copy of the full report should they want one.

## ... and that other significant audience

Sometimes there may be a significant and more immediate target audience that may have a powerful influence on you as a writer: your manager (or their manager and theirs). Anything you write may have to be approved by others senior to you. And because they are senior to you they will, in all probability, clearly know best. Their style may fashion your style. Of course, if your manager writes well this can usefully improve your writing skills.

However, if they are motivated by the need to know best and to keep you firmly in your place, then even a stroll in the park will become a treacherous mountain climbing expedition. There is little I can do about that other than to encourage you to suggest a change of heart in their motivation (in your Sunday best caring, sharing way). And hope that you see the three lemons fall sweetly into line in their eyes.

# Getting started

# Chapter 3 – Getting started

*'What is written without effort is generally read without pleasure'*

Dr Johnson

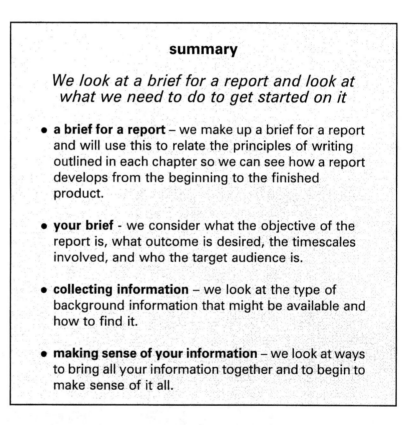

**summary**

*We look at a brief for a report and look at what we need to do to get started on it*

- **a brief for a report** – we make up a brief for a report and will use this to relate the principles of writing outlined in each chapter so we can see how a report develops from the beginning to the finished product.

- **your brief** - we consider what the objective of the report is, what outcome is desired, the timescales involved, and who the target audience is.

- **collecting information** – we look at the type of background information that might be available and how to find it.

- **making sense of your information** – we look at ways to bring all your information together and to begin to make sense of it all.

**your report**

The principles of getting started will be illustrated by applying them to a brief to write a report.

You have been asked to write a report updating your department's progress on carrying out the council's principles of customer care. Let's check out your brief by answering the all-important three questions, covered in the last chapter.

**why are you writing it**

You've been asked to by your manager, who has to present a report to the social services committee but is unable to find the time to write it. So you've got the nod and you're off the subs bench.

*your objective*

Your *objective* with this report is to find out how successful your department has been to date in carrying out the council's customer care policy, and what needs to be done to improve things. It's a *'where are we now and what do we need to do to get where we want to be?'* report. The government's Best Value initiative is stalking the corridors of power and has become the director's close, personal friend. So you had better link it in somehow.

*timescale*

The final document needs to go to a committee date scheduled in three weeks' time. However, the report needs to be with the council's committee section a week before the meeting, so it can be printed as part of the committee agenda. Also, it is intended that the report will be circulated to heads of department and senior management in the department for comment a week before the report is sent to the committee section. This gives you **one week** – in among the things you do in your own job, of course.

Remember that if you don't type yourself (can't type? won't type!) you will need to think about how much time will be needed by the person who does your typing, allowing also time for typing corrections and redrafts. This tight deadline gives you little opportunity to spend a lot of time on researching, organising and writing the report.

**what do you want to achieve?**

You want to raise the profile of customer care and reinforce its importance across the department and council as a whole (or in managementspeak: *enhance its status on the corporate agenda*) and recommend the way forward. You feel good about customer care and you want to promote it – so you will need to think positively about the content and design of the report.

**who are you writing for?**

This report is aimed at members of the committee. However, it is more immediately aimed at your manager, who has the departmental lead on customer care, and who will ultimately present it as a committee item. It will also be circulated to your organisation's department heads and other senior management for comments.

Your brief is short but clear and allows you a degree of flexibility. So, how to get started on the report? First of all, you need to collect all the necessary background information.

**collecting information**

The key information you need is:

- *a timetable for the report*
- *a copy of the principles of your council's customer care policy*
- *copy of the principles of Best Value*
- *an update from each division in the department outlining progress made on each customer care principle*
- *general information on customer care*

**your timetable**

It's important to work out how much time you can (or need) to allocate to the report. Given the report's tight timescale, you need to make sure that any time you set aside is used productively. This means that you need to allocate your time.

There are several time planning or time management computer software packages available – they probably have the words such as *calendar*, *outlook*, and *agenda* in their title. (There are probably even some that help you plan which time planning package best suits your needs). You may already use or have access to one. If you're comfortable with that approach, then fine. You're probably already fully equipped with *management signposting* techniques and will insert *key milestones* as a matter of course. However, pen-oriented operatives might need to do this manually on a sheet of paper or in diaries.

**request information**

***background documents***

If you're writing a report, it's important to get any relevant background documents. These might include past reports, correspondence, guidance documents and so on. In the case of the customer care report. You will need a copy of the council's customer care principles and a copy of the principles of Best Value.

You may have these around your office. Certainly your manager should have copies of these. The fact that you didn't know that the council had adopted principles of customer care as policy and that you have to ask your manager for a copy of them, probably tells you a lot about your organisation's commitment to customer care. You discover that the council has six principles, and that these are:

- *publish a complaints procedure*
- *set and publish standards for each service*

- *actively seek the views of customers and staff*
- *provide services that are fair and accessible to all*
- *explain our services and keep people informed of what is happening*
- *review our services regularly*

Similarly, the Best Value principles are best requested from your manager, who in an attempt to endear themself to the director has no doubt learnt them by heart.

**write to heads of division**

The only way you can write with authority on the current state of play within your organisation is to ask each head of division for a summary report on progress to date. Unfortunately most organisations are hierarchical. An indiscriminate, sweeping, blanket generalisation in the broadbrush style, I know, but needs must. Nonetheless, it usually means that you can expect a prompt response only from those of equal or inferior status to yourself. Pond life can wait.

So, it is probably better, in this case, that your manager's name is attached to this request for information. You should make clear the purpose of your request and the deadline for responses to make sure the information makes the final report. Below is a translation of the type of terms used to encourage a prompt response.

| term used by sender | what it means to the recipient |
| --- | --- |
| please reply as soon as possible | sometime within this decade |
| time limited response required | file to bottom of your in-tray |
| priority one | file to bottom of somebody else's in-tray |
| urgent | within the next two weeks |
| very urgent | within the next two weeks, please |
| extremely urgent | I'm sorry, I never received it |

***general information***

If time is in a generous mood you might be able to research your subject beyond what you know. This gives you a chance to learn (no mean outcome in itself) about the subject, its potential and its implications through:

- *background reading*
- *the experience of others*
- *consultation.*

**background reading**

*new and current books*

The idea of customer care is still a relatively new kid on the social care block. It's a blood relative of those other newcomers – quality (growing up fast) and communications (well, the less said about this, the better). This means that there may be a number of current and relevant books available on the subject.

If you want to check out current availability of specialised books, and your budgets (either work or personal) are nodding away excitedly, then you could contact social and health care publishers for their catalogues.

*libraries*

Alternatively, you could try your local library who may stock or will be able to get hold of books on the subject of customer care generally. Most libraries will only carry lists of books stocked in their particular local authority. However, a good idea is to check the bibliography or reference material in each book. If there's something that interests you and it is not held locally, your library should be able to order any book through the British Library. There is a small charge for this service and you may have to wait a few weeks for the book to arrive.

*caredata abstracts*

A valuable resource is also the *caredata abstracts* published monthly by the National Institute of Social Work. This lists subjects discussed in articles from a wide range of journals, books and reports.

**the experience of others**

*other care organisations*

It is also worth contacting other organisations similar to your own (for example, social services departments, voluntary organisations, health trusts, health authorities) to see if they have anything that might be useful to you.

One of the most overworked phrases I've come across in social care is: 'there's no point re-inventing the wheel'. Tiresome (sorry), as this is, you can't fault the logic. If somebody else has already done it well enough, there's little point in you itching to start from scratch. If you do use other people's work as the basis for your own, or if you simply stick your logo over theirs, or tipp-ex out their name and insert yours, then at least have the decency to credit them.

'If you steal from one author it's plagiarism; if you steal from many, it's research'
*Wilson Mizner*

It can be very useful drawing on the experience of those who were off out of their blocks and around the track even before your organisation found the changing rooms. Learning from others generally means that their mistakes won't be your mistakes – or at least that's the theory.

Private care organisations may be less willing to share information with you. They might only have invested limited time and money (and why should you profit from that?) but as they need to survive in a competitive marketplace they may see sharing as counter-productive, you can but try.

In the case of customer care, organisations might have policy documents, guidelines or procedures for staff, publicity material, annual reports, and so on which they may be willing to share with you. Any material like this may help.

### non-care organisations

There might also be some value in talking to private organisations outside social and health care. In 1991, I was setting up some courses on a social services department's complaints procedure and wanted to link it in with customer care. I did a straw poll of about 30 staff asking them which places they would feel most comfortable complaining to. All bar one (who said *Tesco*) said *Marks & Spencer* (even though most of them hadn't actually ever complained there).

I wrote to Marks & Spencer asking if they could help in some way with our courses – talking to course participants, sending information about their staff courses or inviting me on one of their customer care courses. Unfortunately they (very politely) declined to help. But I think the principle of trying to involve or learn from commercial businesses in certain aspects of our work is sound, even given the differences.

### your own organisation's resources

You never know what information your own organisation has available. Try senior management (or anybody with their own office) as they have a statutory duty to display a glass-fronted book cabinet (look behind the piles of committee papers, family photos and tissue boxes and you may find a book). Try your training or personnel sections. Try any section or person that has the word 'quality' attached to it or them: they seem to have little problem getting book purchases through the system. Try, even, your Chief Executive's Department. You might be pleasantly surprised by what's available. On the other hand, of course, you might not be surprised at all.

### so, what information have you got?

For the purpose of our customer care report, you have:

- got copies of the customer care principles and Best Value principles
- trawled the department's book cases, cabinets and shelves and

have turned up nothing of note other than the skiing holiday brochures of the head of children's services
- written to the three heads of division and received their responses
- trawled other sections and departments.

Now all you have to do is start making sense of it all.

## making sense of the information

If you have ever sat exams that required essay answers, you were probably advised not to launch straight into your answer but to take a few minutes to make some notes, to help organise your answer. This is simply planning your outline. It helps you decide what things you need to cover in your report. It's a tool to help you then decide what's important and what isn't. We're going to look briefly at some ways of doing this. It's important to say that none of these methods are particularly better than others. The best method is one that suits you. You may have your own method that works for you but which is not covered here. That's fine: if it ain't broke, don't fix it.

**skeleton outline**

A skeleton outline requires *brainstorming* your subject. Brainstorming is another buzzword to get managers and would-be-managers licking their lips. It's a strange term to use since a brainstorm means that you are unable to think sensibly and start doing things you would never normally do. On second thoughts, given some of the managers I know, perhaps the term is not so strange after all.

Actually, as any self-respecting flipchart operative knows full well, brainstorming is a well established social work phrase. It is the method of thinking intensively about the subject and getting everything down that you can think of that's related to it. This will be in random order. Your intention is to organise it after you've written it.

Skeleton outlines can take the form of just writing headings, ideas or thoughts as they come to you. Don't worry about what it looks like – nobody else is going to see it. You can always re-write a neater version if you need to. After you've written everything down, you can start to bring the information together. You can do this by numbering your main points (headings may also help) and linking the relevant bits of information to them. An example is shown on page 24.

**other methods**

Make no bones about it, there are other methods similar to skeleton outlines: examples are mind-mapping, pattern notes

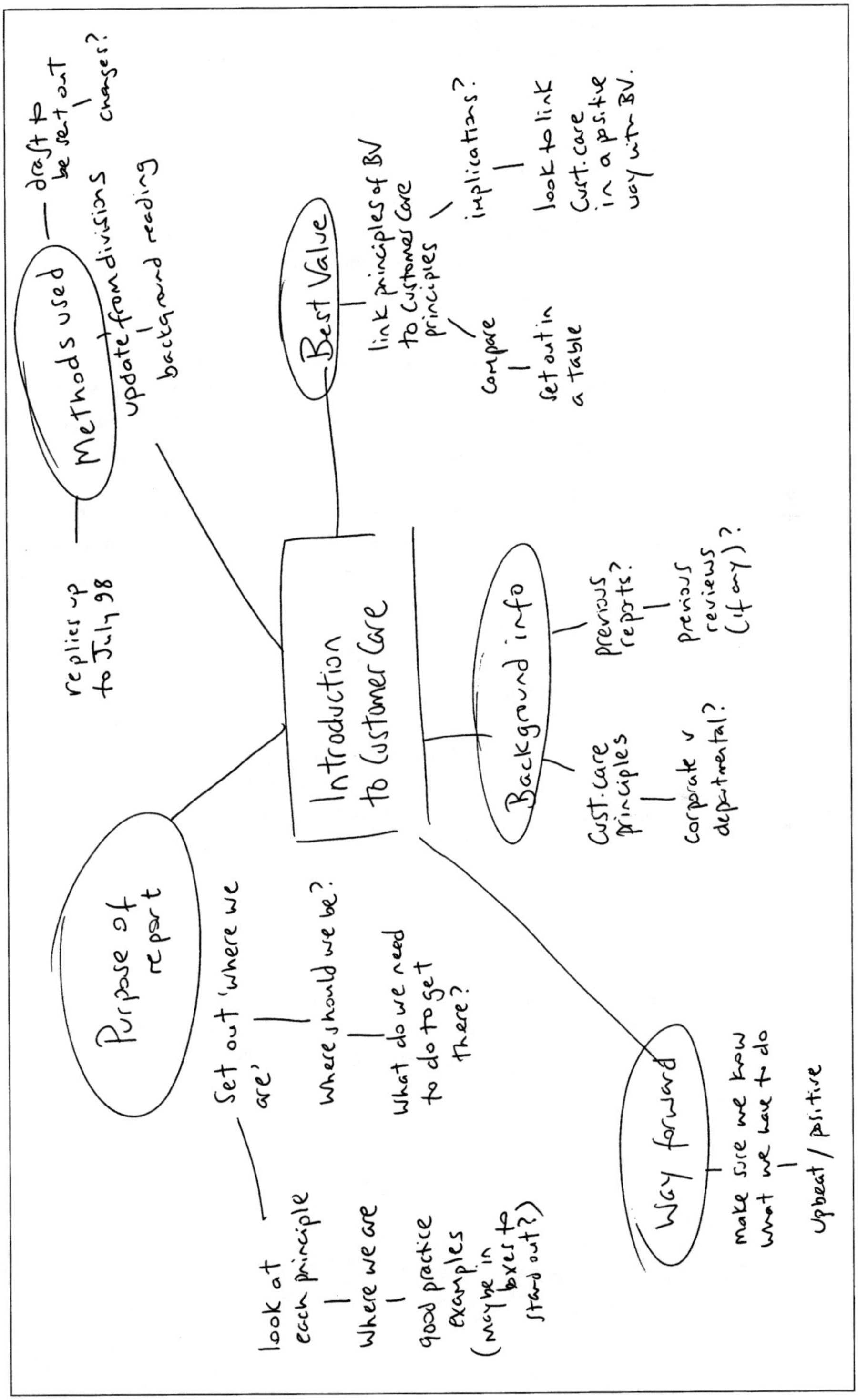
Introduction to Customer Care
Methods used
update from divisions
background reading
replies up to July 98
draft to be set out
changes?
Best Value
link principles of BV to Customer Care principles
compare
set out in a table
implications?
look to link Cust. care in a positive way with BV.
Background info
Cust. care principles
corporate v departmental?
previous reports?
previous reviews (if any)?
Purpose of report
Set out 'where we are'
Where should we be?
What do we need to do to get there?
look at each principle
where we are
good practice examples (maybe in boxes to stand out?)
Way forward
Make sure we know what we have to do
upbeat / positive

*This is an example of a skeleton outline of the introduction to our proposed report on Customer Care.*

and planning trees. You still write down ideas as they come to you but these methods cause you to think about how your information should be organised from the start. A **mind map** starts off with the subject circled in the middle of the page and lines are drawn out to link in main groups of ideas which, in turn, are then linked to other ideas that follow from them. This is also known as a spider diagram. A **pattern note** devised by the Open University is similar to a mind map and again helps to order the information from the start. **Planning trees** adopt the same principle but take on a more structured approach.

Also, I have it on good authority that computer-based outline packages can be a great help (can I have my fee now, Mr Gates?). But I have not used one. Alternatively, you might prefer just to make notes from your background reading.

*making notes*

Another method is just to make notes as you go along: putting down all the information you feel to be relevant. It's helpful to make each new point on a new line so all information is distinct. This is a more detailed approach than the others and allows you to be able to express thoughts and ideas more fully at an early stage. Some of your notes might make your final report with little or no amendment.

Once you've finished your research you can read over your notes to pick out the themes. It might help to list the areas you think need to be covered in your report and number each of them. For example, 1 = introduction, 2 = best value, and so on. Once you have done this, you can go through your notes and number each point to coincide with your list. This will help you bring all the relevant points together.

### and then . . .

'To find a form that accommodates the mess, that is the task . . . now'
*Samuel Beckett*

With all your information gathered and your outline now taking shape, it's time to look at the structure of your report.

# Structure

# Chapter 4 – Structure

*'A place for everything, and everything in its place'*

Samuel Smiles

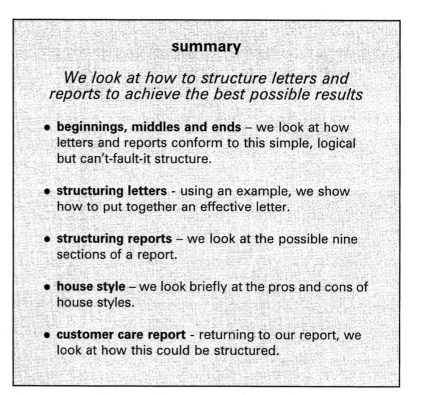

**summary**

*We look at how to structure letters and reports to achieve the best possible results*

- **beginnings, middles and ends** – we look at how letters and reports conform to this simple, logical but can't-fault-it structure.

- **structuring letters** - using an example, we show how to put together an effective letter.

- **structuring reports** – we look at the possible nine sections of a report.

- **house style** – we look briefly at the pros and cons of house styles.

- **customer care report** - returning to our report, we look at how this could be structured.

## introduction

*'Style and structure are the essence of a book'*
*Vladimir Nabakov*

The structure of a letter, memo or report is how the parts of it are organised as a whole – basically, what goes where (and why). A well-structured piece of writing will move through its points in a clear, logical fashion, helping the reader along the way. You will find it easier to structure your letter, memo or report if, as the last two chapters have emphasised, you know your purpose for writing, what you want to achieve and who your target audience is.

Most things you write will have a basic three part structure: a beginning, a middle and (whisper it) an end. In this chapter, we're going to look how to structure a letter and a report.

## structuring a letter

There's something special about a letter. Even if, by today's standards, a letter is by no means the most effective, quickest or cheapest method of communication, it still holds a position of dignity. It's a sort of life president of communication. It must have something to do with its age: letters have been around for centuries; faxes and e-mails weren't even a circuit-tester in their inventors' tool box while the letter was posting its claim to supremacy.

And with its venerable age and status comes the inevitable baggage of convention. We shouldn't always bow to the intimidating power of convention, nor though should it be ignored recklessly. It is the fear of convention that worries people about how to present things in the 'right' way. To get it 'wrong' is to risk social and business humiliation and be cast as ignorant and unimportant.

I've come across complaints procedures that either insist or encourage complainants to put their concerns in writing. Somehow this makes it a more important concern; if you feel that strongly about it, why don't you put it writing? However, people can be reluctant to do so because they feel they will get it 'wrong', have little faith in their ability or are unable to spare the time.

By requiring people to write something you are effectively putting obstacles in their way. Of course, this may be the reason they do it – to discourage complaints. Many complaints procedures, to be fair, do encourage and welcome verbal complaints as much as written ones. Indeed, good procedures will require complaints officers (or *customer services managers* or *dissatisfaction rectification technicians* or whoever) to put in writing what they have understood the complaints to be and send that to the complainant. This is important because we do like to have something in writing, confirming conversations, decisions, advice or information.

If you are to write a letter, you should organise your information into three sections:

- beginning – *greeting, introduction and heading*
- middle – *main body of the letter*
- end – *conclusion and sign off*

**the beginning**

You should make clear in your introduction what your letter is about. This helps the reader identify straightaway the subject of your letter and your reason for writing. Your reader will be able to decide what to do with your letter: carry on reading, leave it until later, pass it on to someone else or see how small they can scrunch it up. A heading, placed between the greeting and the opening sentence, is helpful at the top of the page:

the greeting, title and
opening line

> *Dear Mr Boateng*
> ### *List of nursing homes*
> *Thank you for your letter dated 26 June 1998.*

The opening sentence also helps set the tone for the letter. The example above, by thanking Mr Boateng for his letter, presents a polite, conciliatory and friendly tone. This should, perhaps, be the way we write nearly all our letters, even from people who are complaining. For example, a simple *'Thank you for phoning us with your concerns about the delay in waiting for your walk-in shower to be fitted'* may help to calm the reader. It will help them feel that their point of view is valued and that someone is listening.

The opening sentence should, in most cases, provide a gentle lead-in to the main purpose of the letter. If you are writing in reply to a letter, visit or conversation, you have the very useful *'Thank you for your letter . . .'* introduction. This eases your reader into your letter. If you have to originate a letter then you might try the *'I'm writing to you'* approach. You can argue that this is unnecessary because it's obvious that you're writing to them. However, it is a good lead-in and it's harmless enough. It must surely be preferable to write:

> *'Dear Ms Hall*
> *I'm writing to let you know that we're reviewing our complaints procedure and want to find out about the experience people have had who have gone through our procedure'.*

Rather than the abrupt in-your-face:

> *'Dear Ms Hall*
> *This council is reviewing the effectiveness of its complaints procedure . . .'*

**middle**

The middle or main body of a letter will move through the points or arguments you want to make. Sometimes this is easier if you are replying to another letter – as the points raised in that letter will give you a structure to follow. Our letter to Mr Boateng might continue:

the body of the letter

> *I'm sorry to say that we don't actually deal with nursing homes, as this is the responsibility of the health authority. However, I have spoken to Pauline Telfer, who is the nursing homes registration manager, and she said that they are just reprinting their lists at the moment. But she promised to send you one out in the next few days.*

This letter informs Mr Boateng that his request for a list of nursing homes went to the wrong place. However, the writer has not only informed Mr Boateng where he can find the list but has spoken to the person responsible and organised a copy to be sent out. This saves poor old Mr B having to send out another letter and possibly having to wait a lot longer than necessary.

**end**

Quite often we use the end of a letter to reinforce the purpose of the letter, to make sure that the reader is clear about what will happen or what is expected. However, our example uses the concluding remarks to offer help in the future if necessary. This underlines the writer's helpfulness and helps the reader to feel positive about her.

helpful concluding remarks and appropriately informal sign off

> *If there's anything else I can do for you, please feel free to call me and I will be happy to see what I can do.*
>
> *Best wishes*
>
> *Maggie Hedman*

The whole letter has been helpful and positive. Even the preference for the phrase 'please feel free' is positive, rather than the more usual 'please do not hesitate' which includes the negative word 'not'. Ending the letter with 'Best wishes' reinforces the friendly tone, as does signing her letter with her first and last names.

## a word on memos

A memo (short for memorandum – which is Latin for *thing to be remembered*) is a note sent by a person or a department to another within an organisation. Basically, it's an internal letter. Although my Shorter Oxford English Dictionary regards *memo* only as a colloquial word, both my Chambers and Collins dictionaries give full word status to *memo*. I think *memorandum* is too formal. I have always preferred *memo* but my administrators seemed to fear defying convention more than defying their manager and stubbornly stuck with *memorandum* whenever they sensed my defences were down. At least memorandum is preferable to *InterOffice Memorandum* or the sad and pseudie *Communiqué*.

As it's a Latin word, there are those who say that the plural should be memoranda and not memorandums. However, both are correct as memorandum is now a fully fledged English word and therefore takes the fully fledged English ending of 's' as well as the Latin 'a'. And I always prefer English to Latin. However, Godfrey Howard in *The Good English Guide*, suggests that because '*memorandum* is formal anyway, you might as well go all the way and use the Latinate plural *memoranda*'. None the less, we'll stick to *memo* and *memos*.

## structuring a report

Depending on the length and content of a report it can have anything up to nine sections. Any report you write will be able to use some or all of these:

the beginning

- cover or title page
- contents
- summary
- introduction
- summary of recommendations

the middle
- main body of report

the end
- conclusions
- appendices or extra information
- glossary

We'll look at each of these in turn.

**cover or title page**

See also chapter 8 *Layout*

A short report won't necessarily need a separate cover but should have a title page. Your title should explain clearly what the report is about and in as few words as possible. But not so few that make it anyone's guess what it's all about. For example, prefer *The Implications of the Government's Best Value Initiative for Highfield City Social Services in 1998* to something less specific such as *Best Value*. The first title may not cause your heart to leap but at least it's precise and clear; the second could be anything: a study of the government's Best Value principles, Tesco's top ten offers this month . . . we could speculate for weeks.

Sometimes, and again if the report merits it, you could have a catchy, quirky, bright slogan title that captures the mood of what your report says, but with an explanatory sub-title. I'm fond of this approach and use it whenever possible: ***The Write Stuff*** *– a guide to effective writing in social care and related services*, for example. As Head of Inspection at the London Borough of Barking & Dagenham, we published a booklet that explained our work. It was called ***Accounting for Taste*** *– the work of the social services inspection unit*. We called another document ***An Inspector Calls*** *– standards for the inspection process in Barking and Dagenham*.

The cover or title page could also include:

- the author's name
- the date (a detail that is surprisingly missing from many reports)
- your organisation's name or logo
- version number
- the report's status (draft, final and so on)
- name of department
- contact details

If you're using a cover it is usually best to keep it as uncluttered as possible – especially if you're using a graphic, illustration or picture. 'Less is more' may be the message but just make sure that your 'less' is enough. And I think that just about covers it.

### contents

See also chapter 8 *Layout*

A contents list is very useful, if not essential, in a long report. Your aim (here he goes again) is to make things easy for your reader. A contents page does just that. It helps readers who scan reports to pick out the areas that most interest them. It's an at-a-glance guide to the report and helps the reader become familiar quickly with the report. Just make sure that it is easy to follow.

### summary

Regardless of the size of the report, it is always a good idea to have a summary. People regularly call this an *executive summary* for good reasons I have yet to discover. It is a wasted word that serves no purpose and is as relevant as an executive washroom is to public services. Throw away your key.

A summary will help your reader. It will tell them the main findings and conclusions of the report. It's a snapshot of the report. Busy people have to make judgements about how to use their seemingly ever decreasing time in the most productive way. Your report will be vying for their attention in a very full in-tray. It will also help the reader decide whether they actually need to read the whole report, just parts of it or whether the summary is sufficient for their purposes.

A good summary is never easy to write. It takes time and thought, and is a good discipline for a writer to learn. After all, you are trying to sum up perhaps days of work and thousands of words in less than a side of A4. And you should try to restrict yourself to a page.

I prefer a summary to be at the front of a report following (if needed) the contents page. It ought to be the first thing your reader comes across when they open your report. I prefer it up front so I know exactly what to expect from a report. I can then decide whether to read on. This could be because I'm interested in the subject (through choice or need). Or that I've had my interest whetted by the findings. Or my curiosity has been sparked about how and why the writer came to their conclusion(s). Some people prefer to put the summary towards the back of a report. I'm not convinced about this. I shouldn't have to read a 20 page report and then after I found out what it's all about have it summarised for me.

A report is not like a novel – we shouldn't save all the twists, outcomes and best bits for the last page. For example, a phrase such as 'The £2 million overspend is clearly the fault of the Director's financial mismanagement' should be the first thing we read and not the last.

If you think of newspaper stories they always give you the most important information first and then follow that with the next most important and so on. The same principle should apply to your report. Similarly, the structure of your summary should also follow suit – giving the biggest information first. Sometimes a summary is compared to a film trailer – full of the best bits. However, your summary should also give the plot away (provided, of course, you haven't lost it during the report). Help the reader. Time is short. So make your summary shorter.

Academics seem to prefer to call their summaries *abstracts* because they abstract (take out) the main points. However, *abstract* is a word that is more commonly understood to mean 'difficult, vague, not practical'. This may help explain why academics prefer the word. The rest of us should prefer *Summary*.

See chapter 7 *Writing it*

We will look in more detail at the physical process of writing later on, but it's worth mentioning here that you don't have to write your report in the order you structure it. You don't have to write your summary first, your introduction second and so on. Indeed, there is a very good case (a leather bound, silver buckled case at that) for writing the summary last.

Although you may have a good idea of what your report will say, often that idea won't be as well rounded at the start as it will be after you have written your report. Sometimes during the writing of a report you develop a different slant to an argument, or add to or take away from your planned text. This may affect the report's message and as such may affect the accuracy and slant of your summary. Most of this book's chapters begin with a summary. Each one was the last thing written for each chapter. This meant that I could read back over the chapters and pick out the main points with precision.

It's important that your summary only includes essential information about your findings, conclusion and proposals or options for the way forward. Quite often information appears in a summary that is best suited to an introduction. And now, ladies and gentlemen, please put your hands together, and give our next section a real Las Vegas welcome . . .

## introduction

The introduction should be concise but should give the reader all the background information to the report. This might include:

- the purpose of the report
- who commissioned it and why
- the brief
- the methods used (or the *methodology* if you're being pompous)
- the people or sources of information involved
- any relevant legal or policy information
- the author's details (if not given elsewhere)
- and any other relevant information that helps set the context or tone of the report

## summary of recommend- ations

Quite often a purpose of your report may be to make recommendations based on your findings about the way forward. If this is the case, it is logical to make these throughout the main body of your report where you make the argument. However, it is also a good idea to collect these together and list them immediately following your summary. This will allow the reader to pick up very quickly what you are suggesting should happen as a consequence of your report.

This section isn't reserved for recommendations only. It could also be called *summary of requirements, summary of commendations,* or *summary of options*. Or, indeed, any combination of the above.

Whereas a recommendation is a suggestion, a requirement is not up for negotiation. You may need to make requirements, for example, in inspection reports or other regulatory work that is enforceable by law.

On a happier note, you might wish to commend people or practice. For example, if you're auditing, reviewing or inspecting a service it's useful to highlight the good things that are happening. Too often we seem to either take for granted or overlook what is done well. If you see a deserving back – pat it.

You might be presenting a series of options for others to make decisions about. For example, a committee report suggesting alternative ways of carrying out a particular policy or new legislation and the implications of each option.

However, if you're only making a small number of recommendations, requirements or commendations, or presenting few options, then it might be appropriate to put these in the summary rather than in a section on their own. If your report is short, you may not need this section. Or you might choose to leave all recommendations to the end of the report. The choice is yours.

## main body of the report

See chapter 8 *Layout*

This should be your main section where you report your findings. It should house the detail and deliver a logical flow of information. As the longest section, it is useful to sub-divide it with headings and sub-headings. Headings are helpful to the reader on two counts: first, they should signpost clearly the text, highlighting what is where (and as such need to be suitably explanatory); and second, they break up the monotony of text making it easier on the eye.

Headings alert the reader to a particular topic in the report, allowing the reader to move promptly to the sections that are most relevant to them. Headings should be specific, consistent, clear and logical.

There's no punishment attached to using more than three words in a heading. But you should avoid extending them beyond good taste; once your heading moves onto a second line, chances are you're being a touch extravagant.

You should also try to avoid imprecise headings (such as *'miscellaneous'* or *'general'*). Sub-headings should be relevant to the main heading.

## conclusions

More often than not your summary will include your conclusions leaving this section surplus to requirements. However, it can be useful to tie up all loose ends and close up your report neatly. You may, however, conclude otherwise.

## appendices or extra information

Quite often a report has extra information that:

- is incidental to the subject
- is specialised and that may only be of interest to some of your readers
- does not necessarily sit well in the report itself and possibly distracts from the flow of the report
- might include references to (or the actual) documents that you have referred to or based some of your findings on – to give people the chance to test your judgements against it.

Your appendices might also list the findings of research you have carried out: for example, responses to questionnaires or a blank copy of the questionnaire used. You might also list a bibliography, references or other sources of your information or suggest further reading. Please take care to credit what you have used. Harvard is the usually recommended method but any alternative, such as the one we have used in this book, is okay provided it is clear and consistent.

While appendices (or *annexes* if *appendices* is not pompous enough for you) can be a useful addition to your report you should use them sparingly. Too often people flood the appendices with flimsy extra information that is linked in only the vaguest way. They generally do this to bulk out the report, believing that size does matter and that the bigger the report the more important or better it is.

This book does not claim, despite the author's delusions, to be the way, the light and the truth, preferring to suggest rather than to proclaim. But on this issue I will indulge in diktat. If anything, the bigger the report, the bigger the turn off. Only use the pages you *have* to. Take all other information from their homes at dawn and 'disappear' the lot. The international community will be powerless to stop you. However, if Jack Lemmon turns up searching for some missing information, tread carefully.

**glossary**

If you are targeting a wide audience (including, for example, the public) there could be grounds for including a glossary. A glossary is an alphabetical list of words used in your report with explanations of their meanings. This list would include technical terms or legitimate jargon (including the internal names for groups, decision-making bodies and so on) attached to the subject. In social and health care a glossary might include explanations of words or phrases such as care plan, guardian ad litem, supervision, primary health care, inter-agency, continuing care and so on. And, all too inevitably, on.

If your report is for a limited circulation for colleagues who you would expect to understand the specialised language used, then a glossary is less important. If there are only one or two words that would be candidates for a glossary then you can probably explain these in the main body of the text. But, as ever, the rule is make things easier for your reader. So, if you feel your reader will benefit from an explanation of words at the end of your report, then go for the gloss finish.

## influences on structure

**house style**

The suggestions for the structure of your letters and reports might, of course, be redundant if you have a house style to follow. Sometimes organisations will have their own house style. This is a set structure to follow when writing reports, particularly committee reports, and you will be expected to follow this.

However, even with a house style or a recommended approach you may still have to do some work on structure yourself. For example, reports for many social services committees follow a set style which applies to the cover report on the agenda. This cover report summarises the full report which is often presented in full as an appendix to the agenda. This means that you have freedom to structure your report in your way. Also, if your report is a discussion paper, consultation document or internal report then you might also be free from house style restrictions.

It is commendable that many places have a set way of doing things. This encourages consistency, brings a sense of identity, and it can be a great help to the writer. How*(couldn't you just sense this coming?)*ever, sometimes house styles can be outdated products of another age, stiffened by an overbearing formality. They can be awkward, too rigid or over-defined. Sometimes the only thing a house style promotes is the perpetuation of poor practice (and probably a few more *ps* besides).

If you feel your house style:

- *restricts you*
- *is unclear, vague and confusing*
- *is wasteful with unnecessary section headings which must be filled and hang the cost to the environment*

then perhaps you should challenge it. Easier said than done, I know, as the house style way has been the way ever since that celebrated municipal visit by that nice Mr Disraeli (he were a right gentleman and make no mistake). However, it is wise to challenge a set way by demonstrating a positive alternative rather than relying on time-honoured rubbishing techniques. You might just bring the house style down.

**manager's style**

The only other style that might have an influence on your choice of structure belongs to your managers. If they are sticklers with an overwhelming and unstinting belief that they are the only begotten son of the god of What's Right, then you're only torturing yourself reading this modern rubbish. It's dangerous nonsense. Burn this book immediately (remembering, naturally, to buy another copy when either you move or your manager does).

## our customer care report

**what sections will we need for our report?**

If, as suggested in the last chapter, you've been either charting your mind maps, spinning your web diagrams, planting your planning trees or weaving your pattern notes, then it's likely that the structure for your report is already emerging.

For the report we're putting together, we'll take the easy option and say that the structure of our report is not governed by house style or manager. As the report will be short we won't need to make use of a contents page, summary of recommendations, conclusions (these will be in our main body) or appendices. Also, as it is for internal use only, we can leave out the glossary. So, let's look at the sections we *will* need for our report.

Given the information, it seems that our report might only come to about six or seven pages. However, we do want to raise the profile of customer care, so perhaps a **cover page** can be useful. It will promote the importance of the subject. We don't need to think about a design just yet – that can come at the end.

A title for the report is necessary. A catchy phrase followed by a sub-heading (which makes it clear what the report is about) would be effective. Something like: '***Customer First?*** *An update on implementing the principles of customer care in Social Services*'. Or something like: 'Is **Customer First** the last thing on our minds? – *How Social Services are implementing the council's customer care principles*'. However, again we can think more about this later.

All reports should have a **summary**. As the report will be short anyway, our summary needs to be as concise as we can make it. This will be the last thing we write.

Our report has a lot of background information and this can all go in the **introduction**. We need to think about:

- the purpose of the report – why it's being written and what is hoped will come out of it
- information on the council's principles of customer care
- importance of best value
- methods used and who took part

Our main **body of the report** will be reporting on progress made. As there are six principles, it makes sense to sub-divide this section into six sub-sections, each looking at one principle in turn.

The other main section is to think about suggestions for the way forward. This may be a series of recommendations based on the findings.

So, our report structure could look like this:

- 1 Summary
- 2 Introduction
- 3 Where we are – summary
- 4 Where we are – update on the six principles
- 5 The way forward

We can think about renaming these sections later, if we need to. So, we've done our research, taken our notes and figured out the possible structure. We now need to start thinking about writing the report. The next chapter looks at writing style.

Onwards, ever onwards.

# Writing style

# Chapter 5 – Writing style

*'I don't wish to sign my name, though I am afraid everybody will know who the writer is: one's style is one's signature always'*
Oscar Wilde

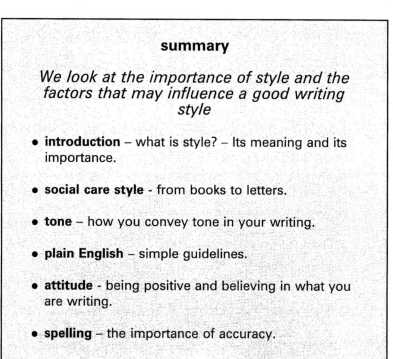

**summary**

*We look at the importance of style and the factors that may influence a good writing style*

- **introduction** – what is style? – Its meaning and its importance.

- **social care style** - from books to letters.

- **tone** – how you convey tone in your writing.

- **plain English** – simple guidelines.

- **attitude** - being positive and believing in what you are writing.

- **spelling** – the importance of accuracy.

## introduction

*'Proper words in proper places make the true definition of style'*
*Jonathan Swift*

Your style of doing something is your way of doing it. So, your writing style is your way of writing something. Style is your way of choosing which words to put together. When you write something we hear your voice, we feel your personality, we touch your soul. Well, maybe a bit over the top but you get the idea.

However, the creative juices that baste your style run thinly when faced with business writing. But it shouldn't dry them up completely – even the dullest task of filling in a log, for example, will still release (or betray) your style.

Writing a book, essay, personal letter or poetry opens up the opportunity to write creatively and show your true style, the real you. But in our jobs we deal each day with the real world and in that world we don't write out referrals as sonnets.

This book is written in an informal, chatty way. Its style is rooted in the wish to inform and guide in a readable, entertaining way. It tries to talk the language that we talk in our everyday lives. It doesn't use an inaccessible academic language that basically translates as 'look at me, I write books'. The whole point of writing is to communicate. How a writer tries to communicate, tries to grab and keep attention is the stuff of style.

Creative writers will (in the main) have a natural, untaught style that is their own. The rest of us struggle to the end of our sentences as best we can. For us, it's more a question of perspiration than inspiration – it's a humdrum, ho-hum, everyday duty. Creative writers might cut their words from the finest cloth, but for us it's all belts and braces stuff.

You might feel that if writing is such a chore then it's only right that the reader should be subjected to the pain, anguish and suffering in reading it that you went through in writing it. This shared-experience strategy, while heart-felt and democratic, does nothing to lift the darkness. We are eternally condemned to pages crammed full of stilted, awkward, overbearing text that promises no daylight for months. Let's see if we can open the curtains . . .

## the write style

The basic idea must be that if I've got some ideas or information that I believe are worth sharing then surely it's my job to communicate them in a clear, simple way. I want my ideas and information to be read. So, I need my words to be readable.

In the first year of my MA in Social Care course, I scored reasonably well on my written assignments but was warned by one assessor, who writes and edits books, to be 'careful with my style'. Another commented that I must have enjoyed writing the assignment as 'the style is almost journalistic!' Yet another said that my piece of work was 'presented in an original style which is **just** within the bounds of academic rigour'. What I was doing (in part) was testing the boundaries in an attempt to (arrogantly) smash single-handedly those very *rigours* of academic writing. I

---

'The most durable thing in writing is style, and style is the most valuable investment a writer can make with his time'
*Raymond Chandler*

'I have called this style the Mandarin style, since it is loved by literary pundits, by those who would make the written word as unlike as possible to the spoken one. It is the style of those writers whose tendency is to make their language convey more than they mean or more than they feel, it is the style of most artists and all humbugs'
*Cyril Connolly*

'An honest tale speeds best when plainly told'
*William Shakespeare*

'Ultimately it's all a matter of style. What it comes down to is this: Do you spell Jennifer with a J or G? That's a class division. As a populist, I'm all for G'
*Gore Vidal*

'Style is the man himself'
*Comte de Buffon*

should have written the assignments in the academic and pompous way expected, but chose deliberately to write in a simple, everyday style. The point of all this is this: a good writer should be able to change their style to suit the target audience.

'All styles are good except the tiresome sort'
*Voltaire*

Sometimes your style might affect your message. An inspector, whose style was to sprinkle as many big words into a report as possible, once wrote that a nursery was *'commissioned* four years ago'. The inspector meant 'opened' but commissioned was a bigger (and therefore *better*) word. Unfortunately for the writer, 'commissioned' does not mean the same as 'opened'. The nursery may have been commissioned 20 years ago, but building only started five years ago and it was opened four years ago. So, the writer looking to be impressive, found the bigger word but lost the meaning.

'Good style is having something to say, having it clearly formulated in the mind or feelings, and saying it, in one's natural voice, in a way that suits the occasion, the purpose and the reader'
*B A Phythian*

It is wise to stick to your natural voice and style. The second you move off into uncharted territory your writing will let you down and you'll be found out. People can easily detect a falseness of style. Don't unpack your gun and go hunting if you would normally pick up your words ready-to-eat from a supermarket. It might seem more challenging to go shooting but more often than not you'll miss. By a mile.

'I know of only one rule: style cannot be too *clear*, too *simple*'
*Stendhal*

'Keeper's done smashing'
*Big Ron Atkinson*

It's important that your style draws attention to your message and not to you. It should help you say look at this, notice that and pick out the other. It shouldn't say look at me, me, me. The message first, the style second. Advice I might do well to take myself. But then when have I ever listened to anybody? Specially me, me, me.

'If imagination can't be taught, the craft of writing can'
*Andrew Motion*

Punctuation and grammar are quite often matters of style or preference. These are covered in *Plain English for Social Services* - pages 5-26.

## tone

Tone relates to the manner in which you do something. When we talk our tone of voice tells others a lot about what we are saying. As does our body language. In writing, the words we use and the way we layout our page sets our tone.

For example, if we want to present ourselves as caring and human we would not adopt the tone of an over-formal, faceless bureaucrat:

> *This Department is in receipt of your correspondence (which was not dated) and have noted the particulars*

*therein. If you care to peruse the enclosed document clients of this Department will be assured that certificated parking licences for the disabled are issued from the Town Hall each weekday between the hours of 0900 and 1645.*

A softer, friendlier tone would make use of pronouns (such as *we, us, our*), everyday and more familiar words and phrases, and run with the occasional *please* and *thank you*:

*Thank you for your letter which I received today.*

*You will be able to pick up your orange badge from the town hall anytime between 9am and 4.45pm. Please find enclosed a leaflet that hopefully explains everything you'll need to know.*
*If I can help in any other way please feel free to call me.*

However, some things need to be more formal. You would not adopt the tone in the second example above, or use contractions (such as *we're, can't, you've*) if you were threatening legal action. And you certainly wouldn't sign off a letter 'With my very best wishes' if you were issuing them with an eviction notice. Your target audience and your message should influence your tone.

We often present minutes of meetings in a standardised and formal way. But this again depends on the audience for your minutes. At most meetings I've ever attended, I don't so much read the minutes as count them. In my old days of full time, regular, paid employment I organised a couple of groups who met four times a year. They were **I**nspection **A**dvisory **G**roups (one for children's services and one for adults' services). They weren't **I**nspector **A**dvisory **G**roups. We deliberately ignored capital letters and made their title a distinctive lower case. We did this partly for style but also to emphasise their open, democratic and informal nature. This group was not to be in the all-important we-know-best-because-we-sit-around-big-tables-in-posh-committee-rooms mould.

I also wanted to avoid the same old faces that dominated social services groups, committees, working parties, panels and whatever. I wanted the public to be part of the groups. It was clear that very few members of the public knew about inspection units and even less knew about the advisory groups. Our remedy? We published both groups' minutes as newsletters and distributed them throughout the borough – to all providers of care, to all voluntary groups, to libraries. It suited the purpose. It raised the groups' profile. It worked.

However, some authorities are less tolerant of such innovation. Or it may not be the authority that is less tolerant but your manager's perception of what is acceptable or appropriate to them or the authority. Once again, you will have to follow suit and just hope you draw a trump card at some stage.

### plain English

I realise that this book is in danger of being little more than a thinly disguised ad for *Plain English for Social Services*. But it is, after all, *The Write Stuff*'s cousin and they are a close family. However, as you might expect – *that* book covers the use of plain English. It's enough her to say that the principles of plain English should also guide your style. These principles are:

- keep your writing clear and concise
- use simple, everyday words
- use short sentences
- avoid jargon
- be positive
- keep your writing vigorous – prefer active verbs (*'the manager intends'*) instead of passive verbs (*'It is the intention of the manager'*).

I guess there are two rules to observe: one, write in plain English; and, two, obey all the rules.

### attitude

Your attitude to what you write could easily be part of the discussion on *tone*. But it's worth isolating it. If you could care less about your subject, argument or message, then the reader will pick this up. And they could care less, too. If *you* can't be bothered, why should they?

Similarly, something that is just 'knocked out' will never compete with something that is well planned, structured and thought-out. Your readers aren't mugs: by treating your words with respect, you're treating your readers with respect. And, in that respect, if you really have no time or effort to spare for something, give the job to someone who has.

### spelling

It is nromal for a book of this knid to talk about the importance of spelling, as this is something a lot of people get incredibly anxious about. The infromation may be the main thing but the quality of spelling does make an impact.

There were four spelling mistakes in the above paragraph – or more correctly – four typing mistakes, which, of course, are not

'A man occupied with
public or other important
business cannot, and need
not, attend to spelling'
*Napoleon Bonaparte*

the same thing. Did you spot all four straightaway? If not, the reason you might have missed one or more is because (and I am a doctor and above the law so I must be believed) your eye is 'reading' the words ahead of your brain. The shape of the mis-typed words are picked up by your eye but are 'corrected' by your brain. All this happens so quickly that you're onto the next sentence without realising that you've put the mistake right. The mistakes above are simple to put right. It is when you come across words that you've rarely or never seen before, or when the sentence structure is complicated or convoluted, that your brain stalls. This is because you're having to work out what's been said.

'My spelling is Wobbly. It's good spelling but it Wobbles, and letters get in the wrong places'
*A A Milne*
*(Winnie-the-Pooh)*

However, trusting other people to miss your typing or spelling mistakes is a dodgy policy. You should really try and do something about it. For example, computers have spell checkers that will hunt out unrecognised spellings. While useful, this method is not perfect. First, the word you have 'mis-spelt' might simply not be in the computer's dictionary (this is particularly the case for words – like *keyworker* – which are part of social care language) - in which case you can add it in. Second, it will only hunt out word spellings it does not recognise: this means that if you mix up a *there* and a *their*, the computer will not 'notice' as it recognises the spelling to be 'correct'. For example the following would be cleared for take-off by a spell-checker:

> *Eye sea know knead two right inn a knew claws too may cower point butt eye am in tent and have know acts to grind, don't ewe no.*

'It's a pity that Chawcer, who had geneyus, was so unedicated; he's the wuss speller I know of'
*C F Browne*
*(Artemus Ward)*

Spell-checkers are not sophisticated enough to be able to judge whether a word is used in the right context. Not yet, anyway. (Why do I get the feeling that the last two sentences are going to seriously date this book?) None the less, they can help you to recognise mistakes and improve your spelling.

Sometimes an added letter to or a missed letter from a world can make a word of difference. I was stirred by a report that talked about 'wok-related' issues and felt impish when a committee report (somewhat spritely) suggested that the awarding of certificates would help 'elf-esteem'.

'They spell it Vinci and pronounce it Vinchy; foreigners always spell better than they pronounce'
*Mark Twain*

The reason you need to spell well is to protect the validity of your work. People will pick out spelling mistakes and use them to rubbish you and your message: 'if you can't even spell *proceed* properly well, what's the point in reading any of this?' Sadly, the world is overpopulated with people like this. They will do anything to undermine you: just don't let them use your spelling

– it's too cheap and easy. Learn how to spell words parrot-fashion if you have to. Also, don't be afraid to ask people how to spell a word (most of the time they will be happy to help, if not only to prove they know how to spell it). And if they don't know either, just think how heart warming that would be. Also, remember that an anagram of *William Shakespeare* is *I am a weakish speller*. But most of all buy a dictionary. And use it.

# Word choice

# Chapter 6 – Word choice

*'No one owns (words) or has a proprietary right to dictate how they will be used'*

Derek Walcott

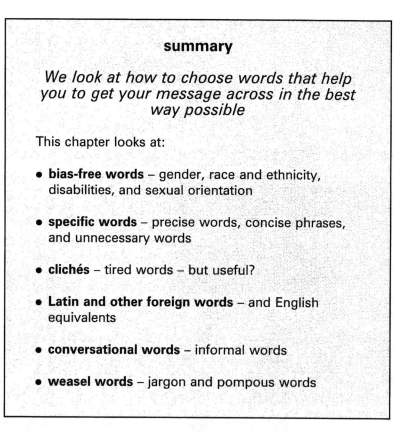

### summary

*We look at how to choose words that help you to get your message across in the best way possible*

This chapter looks at:

- **bias-free words** – gender, race and ethnicity, disabilities, and sexual orientation

- **specific words** – precise words, concise phrases, and unnecessary words

- **clichés** – tired words – but useful?

- **Latin and other foreign words** – and English equivalents

- **conversational words** – informal words

- **weasel words** – jargon and pompous words

**introduction**

Words. There are supposedly about 650,000 English ones in current usage. And if you've read every word up to this point – and if every word was different which, of course, is not the case by miles – you would have come across just 16,000 of them. Zounds.

'The great enemy of clear language is insincerity. When there is a declared gap between one's real and one's declared aims, one turns as it were instinctively to long words and exhausted idioms, like a cuttlefish squirting out ink'
*George Orwell*

'Words are, of course, the most powerful drug used by mankind'
*Rudyard Kipling*

'How often misused words generate misleading thoughts'
*Herbert Spencer*

'Words are chameleons, which reflect the colour of their environment'
*Learned Hand*

One of the things that makes English a dream of a language is that one word might have twenty meanings, and twenty words might (essentially) mean the same thing. This is also the stuff of nightmares.

Words rarely come to us naked. They are clothed in subtleties and carry all sorts of baggage with them. You might mean to say one thing with your words but someone else will hear something else. If we are to communicate effectively with people, we need to choose words that are simple, clear and fit the bill.

Throwaway words can blow back into your face. Gentle words can bruise. Impressive words can deflate. Raw words can cook your goose. Sharp words can blunt your meaning. A word that means this today can mean that tomorrow. It's a minefield out there: your word choice **is** *that* important. So tread carefully.

In this chapter we'll look at:

- bias free words
- specific words
- clichés
- Latin and other foreign words
- conversational words
- weasel words

## bias-free words

**introduction**

This section isn't going to be another mind-numbing lecture on political correctness (or *pc* as it's somewhat disparagingly known). Its public image is not the best. However, do not underestimate the power of words. With so many words available to us, we can be choosy about what we say.

'It seems our fate to be incorrect and in our incorrectness stand'
*Alice Walker*

At the heart of political correctness is respect for and understanding of others. This section will look at the use of language with a sensitivity, tried and tested in the cold light of commonsense. My aim, like that of the Task Force on Bias-Free Language (formed in the USA in 1987) is 'simply to encourage sensitivity to usages that may be imprecise, misleading, and needlessly offensive'.

'We want to create a sort of linguistic Lourdes, where evil and misfortune are dispelled by a dip in the waters of euphemism'
*Robert Hughes*

It is also worth noting that it would be impossible to find writers and readers who will agree on the single best way to say anything. All I can do (or would wish to do) is to raise some of the issues, suggest options and preferences, and leave you to think for yourself and decide which best suits you and your readers' needs. A suitably non-pc cop out, I trust.

## gender

### *gender neutral*

Sexist words are those that either exclude or discriminate against the members of one sex (usually women). We are often told to prefer gender neutral language to help avoiding sexism. This means preferring *headteacher* to headmaster or headmistress, and preferring *police officer* rather than policeman or policewoman. This seems sensible, although there will be times when you will *need* to be gender-specific rather than neutral. Indeed, at times it can seem innocuous or clumsy to deny gender. In everyday life, for example, we inoffensively come across agony aunts, mum's the word, master (as a verb and noun) – none of which are necessarily considered sexist, albeit that the last example presents an interesting conundrum for those Masters of Women's Studies. However, some everyday phrases are considered offensive and should be avoided. For example, old wives' tale, checkout girl, and apron strings.

Despite these more seemingly sensitive times there are still organisations that have a chairman, even when it's a woman. There has been a move towards preferring *chairperson* or *chair* (although my welsh dresser assures me this is furniturist) as more agreeable gender neutral terms. Somehow the ombudsman seems to have survived being turned into an ombudsperson or just plain old ombuds.

### *the singular* they

Acts of law in Britain are written with the generic *he*. For example, this from the first page of the Children Act 1989 (the use of bold is mine and not that of Her Majesty's Stationery Office):

(3) *In the circumstances mentioned in subsection (4), a court shall have regard in particular to –*
  (a) *the ascertainable wishes and feelings of the child concerned (considered in the light of **his** age and understanding);*
  (b) ***his** physical, emotional and educational needs;*
  (c) *the likely effect on **him** of any change in **his** circumstances;*
  (d) ***his** age, sex, background and any characteristics of **his** which the court considers relevant;*

This could be avoided by using the plural pronoun as the singular (in the above example, *him* would become *them*, and *his* would become *their* except the second one in (d) which would become *theirs*). I think that this is a logical progression. This method has already been adopted for laws in Canada. It also helps to avoid all those clumsy 'either or' constructions: she/he; he or she; (s)he; s/he; *and* she (he). The gender neutral plural also leads us to the word *themself*. As in: 'the resident helped themself to a drink'.

This construction has limited support and much opposition. So, if you choose it, brace yourself for the onslaught. But you're probably playing the sea to your opponents' Canute. Time and tide wait for no one.

People who campaign to remove sexism from our language have been lampooned for excesses which were probably not of their making. The idea that every word with *man* in it is inherently sexist is as embarrassing as it is wrong. To suggest, for example, that personfacture (manufacture), personager (manager), ovarimony (testimony) and herstory (history) are suitable non-sexist replacements or female alternatives for sexist terms is nonsense. The first two are derived from the Latin *manus* meaning *hand*. *Testimony* is derived from the Latin *testimonium*, from *testis* (which can mean testicles) but in this case means *witness*. *History* is from the Greek *historia*, from *histor* meaning *knowing*. *Herstory* is just an all too knowing play on words.

Even words that move in perilously close-to-sexist circles can be acceptable in the right context and if it has a counterpart that means the same thing. For example, 'ladies and gentlemen' is an innocent enough phrase to use at celebrations or formal functions. But, perhaps, we should be labelling public washrooms, changing rooms and toilets 'men' and 'women' now. Phrases like 'career women' have no male counterpart. The inference is that it is unusual for a woman to have a career. And should be avoided. The phrase, that is, not the career.

'Whatever women do they must do it twice as good as men to be thought half as good. Luckily, this is not difficult'
*Charlotte Whitton*

The word *matron*, which I can't say in anything other than my best (that is, not very good) Kenneth Williams, is still fairly common currency in health circles (and occasionally can be found alive, well and patrolling the corridors of residential care homes and police stations). Its male counterpart (*patron*) has quite different meanings for us today. My Chambers dictionary gives the following as the third of its three definitions of *matron*: 'any dignified and solemn middle-aged to elderly (especially married) woman'. My Collins dictionary, however, gives this as its first definition: 'a staid or dignified married woman'. The word itself is from the French *matrone*, which itself is based on the Latin *mater*, which means *mother*. Avoid. And prefer *manager* or, if you feel you are constantly fighting losing battles, go for the over-the-top but strangely popular *officer-in-charge*. Forward!

Etymology (the study of the origin of words) should influence the acceptance of words in tandem with modern usage. This will mean that harmless words such as manager, human, and emancipate (which could reasonably only offend the unreasonable) should be left alone. On the other *manus*, there are words that we should either seek alternatives to or simply avoid. A general (and in true job-description-speak *not fully inclusive*) list follows.

**examples of sexist words and phrases, and options for alternatives**

| sexist phrase | *. . . and its alternative* |
|---|---|
| all things to all men | *all things to all people* |
| best man for the job | *best person (or candidate) for the job* |
| businessman | *entrepreneur, executive, professional* |
| busman's holiday | *working holiday* |
| chambermaid | *hotel cleaner, housekeeper* |
| common man | *ordinary person, citizen* |
| craftsman | *craft worker* |
| deliveryman | *courier, delivery person* |
| dinner lady | *canteen worker, kitchen assistant* |
| forefather | *ancestor* |
| gentleman's agreement | *informal (or verbal) agreement* |
| ice cream man | *ice cream seller* |
| laundress | *laundry worker* |
| layman | *layperson, non-expert* |
| maiden name | *own name, family name, birth name* |
| maintenance man | *maintenance worker* |
| male nurse | *nurse (unless gender is relevant)* |
| manageress | *use manager for women and men* |
| manhandle | *treat roughly* |
| man in the street | *ordinary (or average) person in the street* |
| mankind | *people, human race, humanity* |
| manning | *staffing* |
| manpower | *employees, workers, staff, personnel* |
| matron | *manager, officer-in-charge, senior nurse* |
| mother and toddler group | *parent and toddler group, toddler group* |
| mother tongue | *native language, native tongue* |
| office boy/girl | *office assistant* |
| right-hand man | *assistant* |
| undermanned | *understaffed* |

## race and ethnicity

*Race* is used to define people with a particular set of physical characteristics (size, hair, skin colour) thought to be distinct from others. These characteristics are often without scientific base and often exist in the mind of the writer and reader. As there is little agreement about how to class people by race, we should perhaps either avoid or tread carefully.

*Ethnicity* is used to define people who either have or identify with a cultural tradition. Because of its association with, or resembling, what Chambers describes as 'the exotic, especially non-European, racial or tribal group', it carries the idea of being unusual. This is emphasised by the word *ethnic* being sandwiched between the words *minority* and *group*. This is misleading as not all ethnic groups are minorities. Indeed 'whites' are a minority group as far as the world's population is concerned. We should take care with how we seek to label.

We should also take care to avoid words that have a negative colour implication. Again the extreme is to avoid using the word black, period. So we lose *blackboards* (for chalkboards), *it's all down in black and white* (it's all written down) and *black tie affair* (formal evening dress). Admittedly each alternative is acceptable, but should not necessarily be enforceable. The role of the word 'black' in each example is to *describe* an item. It has no other sinister role. How else would I want to describe items of clothing that are black, other than what they are: black trousers, black shoes, and so on? We wouldn't think twice about saying blue jeans. Likewise we shouldn't with black jeans (or *black-black* jeans or *barely-black* tights for that matter).

Other words, though, are not so innocent. Whether or not the etymology is blameless, current usage renders them inappropriate as *black* interprets as something negative, dangerous, sinister or downright bad (blackball, blackleg, black mark, black book, blacken one's name, black sheep of the family, blackguard, black hearted, black magic, black market, black mass, black spot, blackmail, blacklist). *White* in contrast seems to be symbolically represented as *good* (pure as the driven snow) or at least not as bad (white lies, white magic). However, *white feather*, *white flag,* and *whitewash* stain the bleached perfection.

There are few satisfactory answers that will suit everyone on issues of bias-free writing. There will be those black people who wear the label black with pride, and others who will hate being labelled black. There will be those black and white people who will cringe at being asked if they want their coffee 'black or white' and others (black and white) who would not ask in any other way. Me? I drink tea. With milk.

## disabilities

'I feel I'm just like you – I just can't use my arms and legs'.

A disabled man who I employed to carry out inspections of a home for people with disabilities, tells me that once in a pub someone came up to him and asked 'What have you got?' He responded: 'A pint of lager'.

*The Shorter Oxford English Dictionary* defines the word *disability* as 'want of ability; inability, incapacity'. More modern dictionaries suggest more modern definitions: 'a severe physical or mental illness that restricts the way a person lives his or her life' (Collins); 'a condition, such as a physical handicap, that results in partial or complete loss of a person's ability to perform social, occupational, or other everyday activities' (Chambers).

Dictionaries, as shown by Chambers, and the public at large still view people with disabilities as *handicapped* people. Social care more generally distinguishes between the two.

A disability is a physical or mental impairment, but a handicap is something in the physical environment or an attitude that limits the independence of a disabled person. For example, someone who is unable to walk and needs a wheelchair is a disabled person. However, a handicap to this person is that their local pub has no flat level or ramped access and that the toilets are upstairs. Nonetheless, there are disabled people who believe that their disability is caused by society's physical and attitudinal barriers not by any differences in the way their bodies work.

Within social care *disability* is widely accepted. Although there is strong support for *learning difficulty* over *learning disability*. Again the rule must be to ask those who you seek to label: 'what do *you* prefer to be called?'

## able-bodied

'People think I don't have a mind because I use a wheelchair'.

The road we take towards the ideal words exhibition is pot-holed enough that it seems ironic that new, more inclusive language is at times adding to the damage rather than repairing it. The term *able-bodied* is one such hole in the road. Its intention may be inclusiveness but the result is the opposite. Rather than recognise that we *all* have different degrees of ability, it serves only to emphasise the difference between those who are so-named able-bodied and those with disabilities.

Other well-meaning labels such as 'uniquely differently abled' win little support from the people being labelled as such or from the general public.

## disabled people as victims

'I am not a wheelchair **victim** – often my wheelchair is my closest friend'.

Quite often language is used to label disabled people as victims. People don't have cerebral palsy – they are afflicted with it, are victims of it, are suffering from it or stricken with it. All this does is add to the sense of helplessness of disabled people. Also, people tend to talk about disabled people being brave, courageous and heroic when really all they are doing is trying to get on with their everyday lives as best they can. It is patronising, adds to the image of helplessness and should be avoided.

[The quotes used in this section are by disabled people and have been taken from the leaflet *Plain Talking* produced by Capability Scotland (*11 Ellersley Road, Edinburgh, EH12 6HY, phone (0131) 313 5510, fax (0131) 346 1682*).]

**sexual orientation**

*Sexual orientation* is generally preferred to *sexual preference* because most people feel that they don't have a choice about their sexuality.

The term *homosexual* seems to be a combination of the Greek word *homos* (meaning *same*) and the Latin word *sexus* (meaning *sex*). It was thought to only describe homosexual men because it was mistakenly believed that the word was based on the Latin *homo*, meaning *man*. 'Homosexual' can be applied to both women and men. However, many writers look to avoid using the word as it carries a degree of negative criminal and pathological baggage. For example, how often do you hear in news stories about a murderer (or whatever) who happens to be heterosexual? Sexual orientation appears only to be newsworthy if its *deviant* - helps explain it all, you see.

Again, there is no universally accepted way of referring to people's sexual orientation. However, the terms *gay* and *lesbian* come closest. *Gay* is a word that goes back centuries when it meant cheerful, bright and attractive. It still means those things, of course, but is rarely used in those senses anymore. The term *gay* was adopted by the American Gay Liberation movement in the 1960s. It's a word that can also be applied to women (usually in slogans of uniformity, such as *Gay Pride*) but there is a general acceptance that it relates specifically to men.

Same-sex oriented women generally prefer *lesbian*. The word is derived, according to *Chambers*, from the Aegean island, Lesbos, where the Greek poet Sappho (who wrote about same-sex relationships with women – and hence *sapphic*) reputedly lived with her lovers in 7th century BC.

Although words such as queer, fag(got) and dyke, may well be used freely among gay and lesbians themselves, it is considered inappropriate for outsiders. However, such abusive words are slowly being reclaimed (by such organisations as *Queer Nation*) to defeat their pejorative use. The idea being that if the words become embraced as acceptable labels, then they lose their power of insult and abuse. Words are not the only things to be reclaimed either: the pink triangle, once a symbol of Nazi oppression, is now a symbol of pride and freedom. Reclamation is not new. The Quakers and the Methodists, for example, were originally called those names by their detractors as insults to their style of preaching and living.

# specific, definite and concrete words

'When you want to lay it on the line and make sentences clear and immediate, cut out as many abstract nouns as possible'
*Godfrey Howard*

In his book, *The Elements of Style*, William Strunk Jr hits us with both barrels still smoking: 'Prefer the specific to the general, the definite to the vague, the concrete to the abstract'.

'Too many flowers . . . too little fruit'
*Sir Walter Scott*

Abstract nouns (such as *aspect, condition, perception, situation*) are, according to Godfrey Howard in *The Good English Guide*, 'states and concepts we are aware of in our minds but are one step back from tangible objects'. It's no wonder that politicians prefer them. We, however, should heed the advice of Professor Strunk and call it as it is. In this section we'll look at words and phrases that have been used in social and health care writing that could be replaced with something more precise, or with something more concise, or left out altogether. This section should be read alongside Chapters 5, 6 and 7 (Away with Words, Padding, and Everyday Words) in *Plain English for Social Services*.

### be precise

We often use 'catch-all' words and phrases to try cover all eventualities. For example, a children's daycare nursery might only be part of a building or family centre and an inspection report might refer to 'the building' or 'establishment' when it is referring to the whole building. This is useful. However, more often we use these bland general terms when we could be more precise.

| abstract words | precise replacements |
|---|---|
| agency | *say which one* |
| certain circumstances/ situations | *say what they are* |
| communication | *letter, memo, report, talk, speech* |
| correspondence | *letter, memo, report, note* |
| current position/conditions | *delete and say what it is(or what they are)* |
| establishment | *home, nursery, day centre, offices* |
| facility (residential care facility) | *say what (home)- but you can usually delete this word* |

'The reason for preferring the concrete to the abstract is clear. Your purpose must be to make your meaning plain'
*Sir Ernest Gower*

| institution | *building, hospital, prison* |
| organisation | *say which one* |
| passenger vehicle | *mini-bus, van, car, bus, coach* |
| provision (residential care provision) | *say what (home) – but you can usually delete this word* |
| resources | *money (budget), people, time, equipment* |

This is from a social services committee report:

## PURPOSE

The purpose of this report is to inform Elected Members of the current child protection work in general in the Children's Services Division and to further update Members on the changes in legislation together with practice guidance that will further influence and direct future work with children and families in the borough.

This 52 word introduction could be pruned to read like this:

### Purpose

To inform Members on child protection work in the borough and on the changes in legislation and practice guidance that will direct our work with children and families.

The tragic loss of 24 words made no impact on us. We should look to cut back flabby writing in search of meaner, leaner sentences. Here's your recommended diet sheet: listing those flabby phrases and their fat-free alternatives.

'If it can be said at all, it can be said clearly'
*Ludwig Wittgenstein*

| wordy phrase | concise alternative |
|---|---|
| arrive at a conclusion | *conclude, decide* |
| as a consequence | *however* |
| as a matter of course | *regularly, normally* |
| as many as | *up to* |
| as well as | *and* |
| based on the fact that | *because* |
| before very long | *shortly, soon* |
| communicate in writing | *write* |
| fails to recognise | *ignores* |
| for and on behalf of | *for* |
| has an effect (up)on | *affects, influences* |
| in the process of | *in, while* |
| is beneficial to | *benefits* |
| is in keeping with | *agrees with, conforms to (with)* |
| is representative of | *represents* |

'To write simply is as difficult as to be good'
*Somerset Maugham*

| | |
|---|---|
| it goes without saying | *naturally, clearly* |
| it is essential that | *must* |
| not a viable proposition | *can't be done* |
| with reference (regard) (relation) (respect) to | *about* |

**leave it out!**

There are *those occasional* times when *basically* we could *eliminate and* delete words that add nothing *at all* to our sentences. Such as those words in *italics* in the last sentence. The following list gives other examples.

| delete word | as in . . . |
|---|---|
| active | *. . . and is under active consideration.* |
| basic(ally) | *Basically, there are four Divisions in the Social Services Department.* |
| current, currently | *The home is currently managed by Phillipe Clement.* |
| duration | *There was a phased electrical failure of two hours' duration.* |
| entirely | *The nursing home management team were found to be entirely blameless by the inquiry.* |
| facility, facilities | *. . . there was an excellent nursing care home facility.* |
| in general | *The home, in general, is well run.* |
| involved | *. . . with no extra demand on resources involved* |
| positively | *to promote positively – promote means to cause to advance.* |
| the process of | *We are in the process of looking at our tendering arrangements.* |
| to do | *Setting up an advocacy scheme can be expensive to do.* |
| which is, which are | *The care plan dealt with practical issues which are relevant to Mr Burrows.* |
| who was in attendance | *. . . an electrician who was in attendance was unable to restore the main electricity supply.* |

'In the bureaucratic offices of our society inflated sentences are still being written, but the drive towards the use of everyday English in national and local government documents, in legal writing, and elsewhere is gathering momentum'
*Fowler's Modern English Usage*

## clichés

'Not all fixed phrases are necessarily bad'
*Good Word Guide*

It's the same old story isn't it? In a nutshell, we've had all and sundry who, by and large, and with all due respect, can't see beyond the end of their noses. They're in their ivory towers telling us that clichés are nothing to write home about.

I say *hold your horses*. I might rock the boat and ruffle some feathers, but in this day and age, the conventional wisdom smells fishy to me. Indeed, you might think I've got bigger fish to fry or that I've a got a chip on my shoulder, but clichés are meat and drink to me.

'It depends on whether (cliches) are used unthinkingly as reach-me-downs or deliberately chosen as the best means of saying what the writer wants to say'
*Ernest Gowers*

By the same token, and it might be wishful thinking, but there's more to a cliché than meets the eye. Sure, they can stick out like a sore thumb, but mark my words (and let me say this loud and clear) a good, bad or indifferent cliché, time and time again, can warm the cockles of your heart.

I could bang on about this until the cows come home. I know that I'm going against the grain and probably fighting a losing battle (well a cliché isn't exactly a breath of fresh air now is it?) but all things being equal, I want the best of both worlds. And that's not because I'm in two minds either. No, all I say is don't count your chickens (spring, headless or otherwise) before they're hatched.

'A cliché begins as heartfelt, and then its heart sinks'
*Christopher Ricks*

At the end of the day, when all is said and done and the chips are down, a cliché is par for the course. I realise that I've got my work cut out but there's no two ways about it: to some, clichés might stink to high heaven, but I'll use them until hell freezes over. Vive Cliché!

## Latin words

'The safest rule is to stick with plain English unless a foreign expression has no exact or reasonably concise equivalent'
*B A Phythian*

There are Latin words that have become well established in English. For example, *exit* (from *exire* – 'to go out'), *extra* ('outside'), *versus* ('against'), *per cent* (from *per centum* – 'for every hundred), and *ultimatum* (from *ultimus* – 'last'). And there are some that we are stuck with: guardian *ad litem*, census (from *cesere* – 'to assess'), *curriculum* ('a course') and *affidavit* ('he or she has pledged').

'Latinisms have become more often than not out of place and pedantic'
*Godfrey Howard*

But there are stacks that have much plainer English alternatives. Even if the origin of words is interesting (which I think it is) there should be little place for Latinate words in our writing. People who write or speak Latin phrases are probably not only getting them wrong but are probably just showing off. These people say things like the *aurora borealis* rather than say the *northern lights*. It switches me off.

Here are some Latinate words, their meaning and plainer alternatives.

| Latin word | translation | prefer |
|---|---|---|
| ad hoc | for this special purpose | *as and when, now and then* |
| addendum | from *addere* – to add | *supplement, appendix* |
| caveat | let him or her beware | *notice, warning* |

| | | |
|---|---|---|
| de facto | in fact | *actual* |
| erratum | from *errare* – to stray | *error (a more acceptable Latin word)* |
| et cetera (etc) | and so on | *and the rest, and so on* |
| exempli gratia (eg) | for the sake of example | *for example* |
| homo sapiens | wise men | *wrongly used to mean humans – don't use* |
| honorarium (donum) | honorary (gift) | *bonus, gift, donation* |
| id est (ie) | that is to say | *that is (to say)* |
| ignoramus | we are ignorant | *manager* |
| impromptu | in readiness | *spur of the moment, unplanned* |
| in loco parentis | in place of a parent | *legal term (in place of a parent)* |
| in situ | in the place | *in position, carried out while remaining in place* |
| inter alia | among other things | *legal term (among other things)* |
| memorabilia | things for remembering | *souvenirs* |
| per | for, each, by | *for, each, by, out of every, for every, in every* |
| per annum | each year | *each year, yearly, every year* |
| per capita | by heads | *for each person* |
| per procurationem (pp) | by the agency of the other | *by proxy – a stand-in, substitue (when used on letters, prefer for)per se through itself in itself, as such (but usually can be deleted)* |
| pro rata | in proportion | *in proportion* |
| pro tem(pore) | for the time being | *for the time being, at this moment in time, now* |
| proforma | for the sake of form | *form* |
| provisio | from *proviso quod* meaning it being provided that | *a condition* |
| sub judice | under a judge | *legal term, meaning under the consideration of a judge or court and therefore not able to be disclosed or reported on publicly* |
| ultra vires | beyond authority | *outside of one's power or authority* |
| verbatim | using exactly same words | *word-for-word* |
| via | way, road | *by (way of), through* |
| vice versa | the position having been reversed | *the other way (a)round* |

Using so many Latin words in English leads to confusion when it comes to plurals: should we use English plural endings or Latin ones? As ever, there's no simple answer. Some words definitely take a Latin ending (the plural for *basis* is *bases* and not *basises*). However, others can take either a Latin or English ending. Words like crematorium, emporium, ultimatum and memorandum can take either the Latin plural *a* replacing the singular ending *um*. They can also take the simple English ending – by adding an *s*. So you can have *crematoria* or *crematoriums*.

People (usually a manager with only a elementary grasp of Latin, which is enough to be more than most) will probably point out that *agenda* is plural and therefore we should call a single agenda an *agendum*. Agenda is a thoroughly modern English word now. And in English *agenda* is singular. Therefore, the thoroughly modern English plural is *agendas.* That's English the alive and kicking language not the dead and gone Latin one. Also, ask your pedantic colleague do they believe the plural of *rota* is *rotas* (English ending) or *rotae* (Latin ending)? That usually finds them out. If it does, smile smugly and say '*QED*'.

## other foreign words

Of course, it's not just Latin words that feature in the English language. Indeed, English has a very open door policy when it comes to word immigration. If it's a word that works or fills a gap, English welcomes it in with open dictionaries. Time is the only test that words have to pass. *Perestroika* and *glasnost* were two examples of words that filled a niche. However, their usage fell with the Russian empire. We realised it was a niche that didn't need filling after all. So, *perestroika* and *glasnost*, bless 'em, were sent home; no doubt with a flask and a nice packed lunch, but sent on their way all the same.

Some foreign words that are relevant (sort of) to social and health care are listed below.

| foreign word | language | meaning . . . |
| --- | --- | --- |
| bumf | German (*bumfodden*) | toilet paper |
| charisma | Greek | grace |
| commode | French | an ornamental set of drawers* |
| creche | French | manger |
| curriculum vitae (CV) | Latin | course of life |
| ethos | Greek | custom, character |
| liaison | French | link, connection |
| nous | Greek | intellect |
| ombudsman | Swedish | representative |
| paranoid | Greek | beyond mind |
| personnel | French | personal |
| questionnaire | French | set of questions |
| thesis | Greek | a setting down |
| trauma | Greek | wound |

*which could prove embarrassing if, on holiday in France with your incontinent grandparents, you ask the hotel manager if there's a commode you can use.

# conversational words

Conversational or informal words are words that might be subjected to tut-tutting in formal speech or writing. They are also known as colloquial words. The word colloquial comes from the Latin *colloquium* which means *conversation*. It is one of four words used by dictionaries (the others are *informal, slang* and *non-standard*) 'for words and expressions on the wrong side of the tracks' (Godfrey Howard). In solidarity with this book's sentiment to prefer the English word to the Latin, we'll let commonsense prevail and vote for *conversational* and picket *colloquial*.

Formal writers will not pass the time of day with conversational words. But in our type of writing (dependent, as ever, on the context) there is a good case to make use of them. They are words that people speak and as such feel comfortable with. If we are to communicate with our audience, it makes good sense to talk and write to them in a way that they best understand.

There is a tendency to put conversational words in quotes (or speech marks or quotation marks). Professor Strunk would not approve. In *Elements of Style* he wrote: 'If you use a colloquialism – use it'. He added that you shouldn't make it special by putting it in speech marks: 'To do so is to put on airs, as though you were inviting the reader to join you in a select society of those who know better'. People also put conversational words in quotes because, while feeling that the conversational words work best, they are worried what the reader might think about the writer using them. The quotes save face.

Social and health care writing is full of this overuse of quotes. I picked up one report on my desk at random – a riveting missive, from an information technology consultant, grippingly entitled: **Process Review and the Development of an Information Culture – Outline of Key Activities and Tasks for Next Steps** – and scanned for examples. There were a few:

> *On-screen menus are being tailored to help new users 'move around' the system.*

> *. . . the Group will be reviewing the processes within 'provider' services.*

> *. . . focus will be on both 'professional' and 'business' information.*

*If information is seen to disappear into a 'black hole', then nobody will take it seriously.*

It is the sort of stodgy writing that is required (probably by statute) from £850 a day consultants – which is willingly shelled out by social services departments who whinge tirelessly about a lack of money. In each of these examples above (if you can stay awake long enough to read them) the writer could have dropped the quotes, and the only loss would have been ten key strokes.

I was guilty of quote abuse in *Plain English for Social Services*. I've noticed a *'warmer' word* and *the relentlessly 'on-message'* as two examples that, on reflection, should be quote-less. Still, what is life if not a learning experience kind of party thang.

## weasel words

'One of our defects as a nation is a tendency to use what have been called "weasel words". When a weasel sucks eggs the meat is sucked out of the egg. If you use a "weasel word" after another, there is nothing left of the other'
*Theodore Roosevelt*

'The chief merit of language is clearness, and we know that nothing detracts so much from this as do unfamiliar terms'
*Galen (AD 129–99)*

I decided to call this section *weasel words* – a phrase suggested by a friend of mine. It's a term that captures well the type of jargon, gobbledygook and managementspeak that bounces off walls in the offices of middle-management and beyond. Stuff like this:

*In addition, it has been recognised that the successful integration of the CRISSP\* system into the department's key processes will offer a base of sound data together with the effective technology tools from which to develop a full range of information to support and drive the activities of the management team.*

\*an acronym for Client Records In Social Services Programme – a computer records system

This weasels on for 51 words, when all it is trying to say is:
*The use of the CRISSP system will improve the running of the department.*

The use of jargon and pompous language is there to confirm the writer's superior status. You are small beer to their yard of ale.

'For I am Bear of Very Little Brain, and long words Bother me'
*A A Milne (Winnie-the-Pooh)*

Being a weasel is all about making *salient* points. It's about being defensive and never admitting it's your fault in blame-storming sessions. It's about mobile-phonies bashing on about inputs, throughputs, outputs and outcomes. It's about *scoping* a report and not working out what the report should cover. It's about judging cables on the amount of voice and data traffic they manage. It's about developing the watering hole approach and not about testing something first to see how we get on. It's about using empathy when you mean sympathy. It's about seeking out big words to perform the same personal image task that big cars do. It's about putting a positive spin on things (smiling brightly while lying through your teeth so that you can smack others in theirs). It's about adding *-ise* to words in order to make up new words like *diarise*. All of this is weaselling its way into our language and it must be feared.

## Americanisms

Managers spout Americanisms (which can be useful) to prove their status as passport-holding citizens of the world (what they might call *global inclusiveness*). The *bottom line* is a top line for directors of social services and their healthcare equivalent chief executives. The net profit or loss is recorded on the *bottom line* of financial statements, hence the phrase. The bottom line is *the* most important thing for businesses.

'When established idiom clashes with grammar, correctness is on the side of idiom. Put another way, if sticking grimly to rules of grammar makes you *sound* like a pompous pedant, you *are* a pompous pedant'
*William Safire*

Another fave-rave for our leaders is the *ballpark figure*. It's thought to have originated from American TV where the commentators would guess the size of a crowd at a baseball match (*ballpark* referring to a baseball stadium); their guess became the ballpark figure – hence, its meaning to give an idea of what something might cost or how long something might take. Of course, this is not the same as *not being in the same ballpark*. No sirree – as an expression, *not in the same ballpark,* is a whole new ball game, so let's kick it into touch.

Macho American business-speak might well be the only game in town but if we don't get to first base, even with home court advantage, we could be in this for the long haul. Go tell it to the Marines.

## weasels of communications

'Where people arguing politics used to talk of justice, freedom and moral rights and wrongs, the new expertise talks of "parameters", "trade-offs", "interfaces", "inputs", "optimizations", "cost-benefits", and "cross-matrix impact analyses". Nothing is straightforwardly accessible to the layman'
*Theodore Roszak*

Social care has, over recent years embraced/been subjected to* (*please delete as you see fit) commercial business thinking: think of core business planning, quality assurance and control, and compulsory competitive tendering (now dressed up as *best value*). Something else is now skulking around the corridors of power: communications.

It's big business. And it has its own language to prove it. You may well ask – what is communications? Well, I've seen the brochures and I think I can answer that for you. It seems that communications is 'the water in the fish tank'. And not just that, either. It is also the:

- medium for the expression of leadership
- channel for integrating effect
- means to sustain positive energy
- input to decision making.

It's also about integrating mechanisms to achieve a compelling vision which is time-based and loaded with strategic intent. It's about persuasive management, whose task it is to enrol people, convey excitement, sell the vision (no doubt at a discount) and give meaning. Its enemies are meritocracy and institutionalised arrogance. But, perhaps, it's greatest enemy is someone finding out that this is all meaningless bollocks: the obvious painted as abstract. And *that* is the ultimate task of weasel words.

## weasels of recruitment

In my stint in a social services department I witnessed a section go through three name changes. They went from *Staffing* to *Personnel* to *Human Resources*. Interestingly, as the section took on more weasel-like name changes so their emphasis shifted away from staff welfare to becoming a management tool. If they're honest, perhaps they should label themselves the *Hiring, Firing and Retiring (Early) Section*.

'We know that he has . . . the gift of compressing the largest amount of words into the smallest amount of thought'
*Winston Churchill*

This has also resulted in recruitment speak becoming more obscure and ill-defined. This is done partly to make a bog-standard job sound impressive but also to allow for later-date manipulation should the recruitment procedure (strangely) not turn up the quality expected or desired.

So, we get a management development programme talking about a 'framework for a structured approach to human resources development, focusing on equal opportunities as a key manifestation of valuing diversity'. We're all doomed.

'I fear those big words . . .'
*James Joyce (Ulysses)*

Job adverts used to amuse me but now the off-the-shelf, build-your-own approach bemuses me. I think we've all seen jobs advertised like this:

> *You will be a committed, confident, well-motivated, lively, friendly, flexible, innovative self-starter who enjoys working in a dynamic and supportive environment and rises to the daily challenges provided within a hectic team atmosphere, while being able to demonstrate experience of managing change in a turbulent environment along with the enthusiasm, drive, and energy to work with other agencies to provide positive outcomes in a framework of integrated systems geared to providing intensive and flexible services. Good communication skills are essential.*

Previous applicants need not apply.

# Writing it

# Chapter 7 – Writing it

*'Eeyore was saying to himself, "This writing business. Pencils and what-not. Over-rated, if you ask me. Silly stuff. Nothing in it."'*

A A Milne (*Winnie-the-Pooh*)

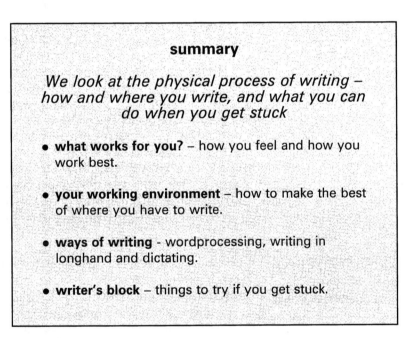

**summary**

*We look at the physical process of writing – how and where you write, and what you can do when you get stuck*

- **what works for you?** – how you feel and how you work best.

- **your working environment** – how to make the best of where you have to write.

- **ways of writing** - wordprocessing, writing in longhand and dictating.

- **writer's block** – things to try if you get stuck.

## write on

**introduction**

In this chapter we're going to look briefly at the factors that influence the physical aspects of writing – the putting of pen to paper or the fingertip to keyboard. This means looking at:

- you
- your working environment
- ways of writing
- writing tactics

### you

How you feel will have a direct impact on the quality of your writing. If you have prepared well, and organised your time, information, structure and layout you will feel relaxed and confident about filling in the gaps with words; an easy join-the-dots exercise. Being relaxed and confident is generally good. Being anxious and uncertain is generally not. But for some people the opposite will be true: being anxious and uncertain can focus the mind to seek quick remedies to such afflictions.

Having organised your time may well help you fine tune (or, indeed, re-tune) your work. Having no time – the report is needed – uh-ho – *yesterday* – 'quality is sacrificed at the altar of speed' (as one nursing homes inspection report actually put it in a 'look, there's the top! Let's go over it!' kind of way). For others it is the looming, all but spent timescale that inspires rather than defeats. Some thrive on the cut and thrust of pressure, others fall helplessly on its sword.

I'm equally at home drowning under pressure as I am with the luxury of dipping my toe in the oceans of time I have to finish something. However, I'm about as much use as a Zanussi refrigerator appliance salesman in the Antartic if I'm tired, uninterested or unsure what's expected. Only you will know what mood is best for you when it comes to writing. Your aim must be to take steps to make sure that you're in that mood as often as possible. There are also other factors to take into account that might influence your ideal way of working. First, and in your face, is the environment you have to work in.

### your working environment

What my working career has failed to chalk up in terms of years, it has made up with variety (at least until I moved into social care). And, the local authority I worked for was the only place I had worked where they tended to look upon having your own desk and chair as a luxury. It was a shared joke of the 'what-are-things-coming-to?' and the 'well-what-do-you-expect?' type in those days. Nowadays, of course, the idea of *hotdesking* – sharing desks – is, well, hot. But having access to a desk or any related flat(ish) surface to write at is perhaps a minimum requirement.

People's working environments can vary greatly: from the dizzy heights of your own office to life in the open-plan auditorium. Again, people differ as to what set-up works for them. The reality is that choice may well not be an issue and we have to make the best of what we've got. But whether you have an office, a cubicle, or open-plan arena, you are constantly on the at-risk-from-distraction register.

The distractions at work can include:

- phone calls
- fax calls (or whatever it is that faxes do)
- e-mail blips
- passing visits (usually by weasels who tell you just how hard they work, although spending all their time telling you about it rather than showing you)
- office chat
- passers-by
- today's post (the temptation of the new)

Of course, you might also work from home. This could be the case if you are allowed to escape office distractions in order to complete a particular piece of work. Or, as happens with an alarming regularity, your office hours simply extend into your home life. Or, as is happening increasingly (at least in the larger county councils) you normally work from home.

Working at home, in any of the above guises, will also have its distractions. Not least the family or others who may live in your house. There's the temptation to do anything but work (the paid variety): the tv is a glance away; the garden (or window box) could do with a bit of tidying up; that play on Radio 4 sounds interesting (well compared to a 20 page report on Community Care Transitional Grant Review and Expenditure Plan, even Martin Day on Essex FM sounds tempting – well, almost), and so on.

At home (and sometimes at work) the obvious temptation is to put on background music, usually the radio. Again, people are different. I find background music at times incredibly helpful and at other times infuriating. I rarely have the radio on as the spoken word (inane or otherwise) distracts me more than just music. The thing, though, is to set your environment as best you can to suit your way of working.

## methods of writing

There are, in the main, three methods of writing:

- wordprocessing
- writing in long hand
- dictating

### *wordprocessing*

The term 'word processor' was coined in the 1960s by IBM to describe its magnetic tape typewriter. Both Chambers and Collins list 'word processor' as two words. Collins also lists 'word processing' as two words, although Chambers does hyphenate them: 'word-processing'. It does seem sensible, and it is *The Write Stuff*'s preferred way, to make both forms one word: *wordprocessor* and *wordprocessing*. Indeed, I'm informed that the 1998 Oxford dictionary has it as one word. After all, we don't write 'type writer' or 'type writing' do we? Since wordprocessing burst onto our screens in a big way in about 1982, it's been a key player in writing. The advantages are that it's quick, efficient, you can create on screen, you're in control and you can present your work in a clear, attractive way.

If you don't type, but are able to, it's certainly worth learning. You will never be able to write in long hand as fast (or as clearly) as typing. It will take you longer to begin with but stick with it and you won't regret it.

### writing in long hand

One down side of relying on keyboards rather than pens is the inevitable deterioration in your handwriting. I used to be a neat writer. I'm just short of illegible now. It's a bad sign when you struggle to understand your own notes and shorthand. Unless, of course, you are a medical student. This means that you are close to graduating.

During the time I was writing this book, I bought myself a fountain pen. I had read many writers who said they couldn't write with anything else. I didn't want to buy an expensive one in case I didn't get on with it. So, I bought, as you do, the second cheapest one that they kept in a glass case. And it was also the only one that didn't have gold on it – a real find in the Essex heartlands, let me tell you. The assistant asked if I would like to try it and then stood staring at the sheet of paper to watch while I used the pen. Caught short of inspiration and under intense pressure from the assistant's stare, I scrawled 'So how does this feel?' My handwriting was embarrassing and I felt obliged to apologise for it. 'Mine's terrible, too,' said the assistant in embarrassed solidarity. It didn't help.

'The trouble with the world is that the stupid are cocksure and the intelligent full of doubt'
*Bertrand Russell*

That's a problem with writing in longhand: legibility. You need to make sure that your typist will be able to read not only your handwriting but understand your shorthand notes. Another problem is time. It takes longer to get to your end product: you write it, a typist types it, you change and correct it, a typist types the changes and corrections, and so on.

Another challenge to legibility is handwritten changes on your handwritten copy. We very rarely write a long piece of work without changing great whacks of it, inserting bits we'd forgotten or just thought of, taking out bits that don't work, moving bits to other parts. All of this adds to the potential confusion for the poor typist who has to make sense of it all.

However, the greatest plus for writing in long hand is that you can hide behind a splurge of ink all those words that you don't spell well – and leave it for your typist to spell correctly.

**dictating**

Dictation is less physical work than typing or writing in longhand, but it is a difficult skill to master. Whenever I've tried it, I found the most useful button on the hand-held recorder was the *rewind*. I kept forgetting what I had said previously or where I was up to, and had to keep going back to check. It was an ultimately dissatisfying and frustrating experience for me, but it might work for you. Try it and see.

However, skilled dictators (if that's the right word) talk it up. It usually means using everyday spoken words so it tends to cut out the pomp of the written word. However, conciseness is often lost. There's also the problem of explaining layout and punctuation. I recall a typist who actually typed in all the punctuation instructions: 'in order to promote open speech marks The Citizen close speech marks we must . . .'

**writing tactics**

In this section, we'll look at some writing tactics: using rough drafts and overcoming writer's block.

**writer's block**

I'm sorry, but I just can't think of anything to put here.

**rough drafts**

Whether you type or use longhand, consider using double-spaced lines. If you're writing on a lined pad, use every other line. This will leave you space to put in changes and comments without having to cramp them in between closely written lines. Also consider only using one side of paper. This means that any additions can be put on the back, with a suitable comment on the front side along the lines of 'insert ❶ overpage here'.

It's good to get everything down, so that you can start fine tuning. Sometimes we're not too sure where our words or thoughts are going to take us until we write them down. Edward Albee's comment 'I write to find out what I'm thinking about' will ring true for many of us.

A rough first draft is usually top secret and for your eyes only – so don't worry about spelling, how it looks, crossing outs and the like, as you can sort that out later.

## writer's block

We will all suffer writer's block at some stage. They say the pen is mightier than the sword. But I swear, at times, a sword would be easier to write with. No matter how hard we try, there are times when we just can't seem to say what we want to say. How often have you written something only to say: 'That's not what I meant'. Or, you simply can't get going, or you can't finish a

That's writer's block, that is. It's nothing special. It's not writing's version of yuppie flu. It's not the exclusive property of novelists or creative writers. It is indiscriminate and can hit you at any

Some things you can try to unblock the block:

- take a walk

- do something else (answer a letter, write a memo, get a life)

- talk to someone about what you're trying to say – quite often as you talk about it, it becomes clearer to you or people will suggest things that crack it for you

- if you're alone (or if have no embarrassment threshold) read out aloud the bits around your blocked area or talk aloud to yourself about what you're trying to say

- go to other, easier parts of your report – you don't have to write anything in any particular order, so come back to the blocked bit later

- put a note along lines of 'need to put something here that leads into the next part' and tackle later with a refreshed mind

- try to relax (use music, go somewhere else, have a drink) as usually tension builds if you have a block and that only adds to your problems

- and then when you think your report least suspects, pounce and catch it off guard, grab the little varmint, shake it by the neck and beat seven bells of shit out of it . . . then begin

Oh, and finally, remember that . . . no, it's gone.

# Layout

# Chapter 8 – Layout

*'I believe in . . . the might of design'*

George Bernard Shaw

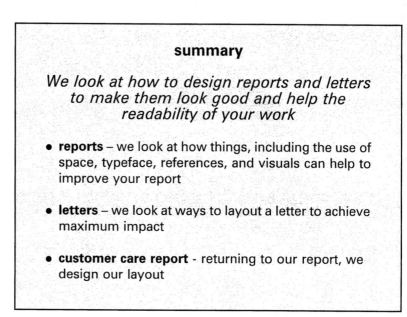

**summary**

*We look at how to design reports and letters to make them look good and help the readability of your work*

- **reports** – we look at how things, including the use of space, typeface, references, and visuals can help to improve your report

- **letters** – we look at ways to layout a letter to achieve maximum impact

- **customer care report** - returning to our report, we design our layout

See chapter 4 *Structure*

**introduction**

Although, clearly, what you have to say is the most important thing, you really shouldn't underestimate the potential effectiveness of a good layout. When somebody picks up your report, letter or memo, the first thing they notice is the design – what it looks like. If your report or letter is set out in a clear, sharp and neat way, this will signal to the reader that your message is similarly clear, sharp and neat. On the other hand, if something is laid out in a confusing, untidy and sloppy way, then so it follows must be the message.

Standard letters that have suffered acute physical abuse at the unforgiving hands of the photocopier often end up shadows of their former selves. The clarity of the type may have been lost making it difficult to read. The page is inevitably skewwhiff, while corners and edges are tainted with unsightly smudge-shadows. The end product that is then posted out gives the impression that nobody cares. This logically leads to the reader caring little, also.

Remember first impressions *do* count. For example, you might dress smartly for a job interview, in order to promote a positive impression of yourself, to which you then will try to confirm through the course of the interview. A well presented report or letter does much the same: the design makes a positive impression on the reader, who has those impressions confirmed by what you have to say.

However, don't worry, you don't need to be Professor Dabhand of the Layout & Design Institute to produce well designed work. All you need is access to a computer and some simple guidelines to help you on your way. We'll look at some things to think about when writing:

- reports
- letters
- memos

### reports

some simple design tips: an expert writes

As clearly the world's paragon of design, people often come over to my table while I'm dining at top restaurants and say to me (understandably nervous while in the presence of greatness): 'if I was laying out a comprehensive report on, oh I don't know, let's say *staff supervision in a turbulent environment*, what advice would you give?'

For starters, I would advise them to jolly well change the title of their report. Unless they *want* their audience to dine elsewhere, of course. Without handing it on a plate for them, I would recommend that they might care to think about:

- covers
- space
- typeface and font
- single or double sided paper
- portrait or landscape
- referencing
- highlighting
- using visuals

covers

We have already looked at the importance of covers. Long reports deserve a cover. Not only does a cover help promote and identify your report, it also protects it from being eared and dog-stained (I think). The cover also says something about your subject, your organisation and you. So, spend some time thinking how it might best look.

If your report is a draft document sent out for comment or is to be circulated to only a few people, then perhaps a glossy, full colour, artboard cover might be *over-egging the parsnips* or something. A paper cover, perhaps in a different colour, will probably do the trick. Below we show four cover designs: a simple cover, a cover using a photograph, a more striking cover and a messy cover.

*Use of photo*                              *Simple cover*

*Striking cover*

*Messy cover*

**think space**

Modern design has recognised the importance of nothing: nothing is good. When laying out your page, think space. It may well be the final frontier, but we're looking to create space not conquer it. Words, in the phrase of psychobabble, need their own space. The more blank (usually white) paper you see, the easier a page is on your eye.

*using colour paper*

Of course, you might not always use white paper but you should prefer it whenever possible. It gives the best contrast to black type. Any other colour paper cannot match the clarity. Some people use different coloured paper for different sections of a long report, in an attempt to improve access: 'the recommendations on how to improve services for less money? You'll find that in the rose tinted section'. This is a bit gimmicky, as a good contents page is usually all you need. Save colour paper for covers (which use little type) and publicity (to help it stand out in a crowd) but not for reports. For people with visual impairments, the Royal National Institute for the Blind recommend white or yellow paper.

By thinking space, you could be thinking about:

- using generous margins
- giving your headings room to breathe
- using vertical lists (like this)
- using short paragraphs
- using visuals.

*using generous margins*

You should aim to have a minimum one inch (2.1cm) margin all around the page. Or at least wide enough to restrict you to using less than 15 words a line. Using more than that will cause your reader to struggle. This book is designed with a wide left margin. This is not only useful for side headings and margin notes but also makes the book much easier on the eye: it makes it look good and makes it easier to read. Away from the aesthetic, using a left hand margin also has a rather spiffing practical application, actually: it means you can bind your report, if necessary.

I held a training course for a county council social services department which produced reports that had a minimal margin – about a centimetre. The council had a laudable policy to save paper and this was one of their ways in which to do so. However, the reports were scary: the sheer expanse of text punched you in the face when you dared look at it. It was too much to deal with, you became bruised and breathless just looking at it. Denying your report a decent set of margins may well save a ream or two over the year, but if nobody reads your report because they can't cope with the design, it will waste not only paper but your time as well. Fence off your page with good boundaries and don't marginalise their importance.

***give headings room to breathe***

Headings, as well as being references or signposts for the reader, help to break up the text. But to do this they need room to breathe, so don't suffocate them with text either side. Prefer something like:

---

2.2 Communication is integral to everyone's daily life and work: what they do and how they do it, no matter the role or task, is dependent on communication.

**3 Why we need good communication**

3.1 Communication is at the core of every organisation. Effective communication is the life force of an organisation enabling it to motivate, empower, influence, inspire, explain, improve and change. As a public organisation, the council also has to be accountable for its decisions and actions.

---

The example has a one line gap between each point and the heading. The indented text for each point also helps create space and improves readability.

The same example, without the space around the heading or the indents would look like this:

---

2.2 Communication is integral to everyone's daily life and work: what they do and how they do it, no matter the role or task, is dependent on communication.
**3 Why we need good communication**
3.1 Communication is at the core of every organisation. Effective communication is the life force of an organisation enabling it to motivate, empower, influence, inspire, explain, improve and change. As a public organisation, the council also has to be accountable for its decisions and actions.

---

The second example is cluttered. By not giving the heading or the text room to breathe, the reader doesn't feel able to pause after each point but is forced through the document. The first example by indenting the text and by providing space around the heading delivers its points in a more compact and organised way. The reader is able to take in the point because the design encourages them to pause and reflect before moving onto the next point or section. This design also helps the reader because it gives them targets to aim for – a very useful device in a long report. And any report should be entitled to be heading in that direction.

## *using vertical lists*

Lists are very useful devices to break up text and to present information in a more readable way. This book uses lists a lot (I do take my own advice now and then). *The Write Stuff*'s chapters include: Introduction; Planning; Structure; Writing style; Word choice; Layout; Editing. This list given as part of continuous text presents the information correctly enough but makes the reader work to pick out all the subjects. Whereas a vertical list helps make each item stand out. Prefer:

*The Write Stuff*'s chapters include:

- Introduction
- Planning
- Structure
- Writing style
- Word choice
- Layout
- Editing

In a vertical list some people would punctuate each item with a semi colon (;) in the same way used in the horizontal list example. The final item would be punctuated by a full stop. Although this method of punctuation is fairly conventional it isn't necessary. The purpose of punctuation is to make your meaning clear. An *un*punctuated horizontal list (introduction planning structure writing style word choice layout editing) would be confusing. However, in a vertical list the bullet point (•) makes clear that each item is separate. You could not possibly read it any other way, so the use of punctuation is, well, pointless.

Some people prefer to substitute numbers, letters or roman numerals for bullet points. However, I prefer to fire shapes at people. I also prefer the round point (something to do with the perfect circle, I suppose). But you may ■ up to me and claim that ◆ ◆ are your best friends. Fine, they do the job just as well. But for me, I would bite the bullet and go for a • every time.

However, all of the above can (and very possibly will) be ignored in the most cheerful of fashions in technical reports. These reports will be aimed at other people well versed in the technicality of it all and who will expect little else. Horses for courses and all that.

**short paragraphs**   In reports, paragraphs tend to be numbered for ease of reference. This quite often has the positive effect of keeping paragraphs short. However, there are still those people who will keep all possible information relating to the same subject matter confined to one paragraph. Provided you are not in mid flight with an argument you should look to keep paragraphs down to an average of four or five sentences. The key word is average. A paragraph can be one sentence upwards. Paragraphs and sentences of varying length (sentences should average between 15 and 20 words) have two positive effects. First, they help keep the reader interested as your writing will be more lively for the variety; and second, it helps with the look of your page.

However, you might find that you have gone on for a number of sentences. For example, the paragraph above has eight sentences. You can often move onto another paragraph courtesy of a transitional word such as *however* - which this one did by the most amazingly contrived coincidence. This allows you to develop the subject but in different paragraphs without losing or confusing your reader. In your battle to improve readability, deploy the paras but keep their missions short and effective.

**typeface and font**   These two printing words used to have distinctive meanings: typeface referring to the shape and style of letters; and font referring to the size of letters. However, with the growing popularity of computers, the two words are now used interchangeably.

Your choice of typeface may be restricted by either your organisation's preferred style or by what your computer can do (but even the most basic software packages offer several typefaces). You should prefer clear and clean typefaces that retain their clarity even after a boilwash in the photocopier. The typefaces available to me include Univers, Times New Roman, Plantin, **Gill** and Garamond. They are all well established and do the job to spec. *The Write Stuff* uses Univers.

Resist the temptation to experiment too much, particularly with *fancy* typefaces which might look good but have little practical use. They might work for advertising the office christmas party but as everyday texts they are too much.

The size of font you choose is measured in points. Each point is 1/72 of one inch. So 12 point is 12/72 or one-sixth of an inch. In general, for writing reports, memos and letters 12 point is adequate. However, prefer a larger font if this will help your target audience. For example, in my last job, letters that were sent out to residents in homes for older people were usually printed in 14 point. It is sometimes useful to use a larger font than your main text for your headings (but stick to the same typeface – mixing those up can be distracting to the reader).

## single or double sided paper

Some organisations have a policy on this, and if yours is one of them, well, that's that. Printing on both sides of paper is environmentally and financially sound. However, having a report that is one-sided (in terms of design rather than point of view) is easier on the eye; as you turn the page you have a blank sheet to offset the typed page. Double-sided can appear too much for a reader and can put them off. So, a single-sided report that is read can be less wasteful than a double-sided report that is filed under 'bin'.

## portrait or landscape

Whatever design tools you may wield (rotating graphics and the like) there are only two ways to hold a page: either straight up like this book (portrait) or on its side (landscape). Portrait is the way most pages are oriented. It is so-called because the page resembles the shape of canvas used for painting portraits. Landscape is so called because it resembles the shape of the canvas used for painting landscapes.

Most things we read use portrait; it's what we feel most comfortable with. Landscape is more awkward: it's difficult to hold which makes turning pages difficult; it gets damaged easier; and, because it's unusual, it leaves your reader unsure about the report altogether. On those rare occasions when a graph or other visual aid (which is *essential* to your report) cannot fit comfortably into portrait, then you have little option to rotate round to landscape (as we did in this book with the example of a skeleton outline on page 24, and a landscaped example on page 87). Landscape is home for spreadsheet specialists, financial fliers, and number crunchers the world over. Leave it to them. If you believe landscape to be beautiful, then take up painting. For report writing, wherever and whenever possible, prefer portrait: for your reader it's head and shoulders above landscape.

## referencing

Numbering your paragraphs and headings is useful, if not essential. It helps the reader to refer to points you have made

quickly and easily. This is particularly the case if you're
circulating the report as a draft for comment or as a consultation
document. If your report marches on bravely past page four,
then numbering your pages also becomes useful. However, if
your report is below ten pages then good, well organised and
clear referencing may well do the business.

In referencing the sections and sub-sections of your report, you
should stick to using numbers (1, 2, 3) as these are most easily
recognised by people. Letters, either upper case (A, B, C) or
lower case (a, b, c), and roman numerals (i, ii, iii) should be
avoided like answering the phone on a Friday at 4.43pm.

Also, remember that your numbering is a *point of reference* so try
to limit sub-divisions of a section to one decimal place (1.3, 4.7,
2.17). Go to two decimal places if you really *have* to (1.2.1, 3.2.6),
but **never** any further, although prefer bullet points if possible.

---

**2 Referencing**
2.1 Good referencing is possible by:
    2.1.1 using numbers
    2.1.2 being consistent
    2.1.3 indenting sub-sections

**2 Referencing**
2.1 Good referencing is possible by:
    • using numbers
    • being consistent
    • indenting sub-sections

---

Any more than two places and, although you are following a
sound logical sequence, the reference becomes less clear.
Something like *23.12.1 (a) iii) (c)* is bordering on the meaningless
but, nonetheless, was found grimacing in a social services
complaints procedure. I was surprised to learn that the
procedure was written by the authority's legal section. Not.

Three final points. First, computers often have automated
numbering. Don't be bullied: override it if it suits not your
preference or purpose. Second, try to avoid the absurdity of
labelling a section 1.0, 2.0 and so on. It is as pointless as the
people who do it. And if anyone tells you otherwise, feel free to
beat them severely with a very blunt instrument; they'll never
find a jury to convict you (unless the jury all work for computer
sections, of course). And, finally, remember you only have, say, a

2.1 if you have a 2.2; if you don't have a 2.2 then your first point is 2 (and not 2.1). In much the same way that we won't in England have a King John I or Queen Victoria I until there is a John II or Victoria II.

**contents pages**     A contents page is a must in a long report. It gives the reader an at-a-glance summary of the sections of a report as well as pinpointing where to find each one. However, I've come across many contents pages that haven't been given the time they deserve. For example:

**INDEX**

|  | **PAGE NO.** |
|---|---|
| **SECTION I** | |
| **About the HOME** | **1** |
| **SECTION II** | |
| **EXECUTIVE SUMMARY** | **2** |
| **SECTION III** | |
| **RECORDS** | **3** |
| **SECTION IV** | |
| **THE ENVIRONMENT** | **6** |
| **SECTION V** | |
| **MAINTENANCE and STRUCTURAL REPAIR** | **9** |

This contents page (wrongly called an *index*) is confusing. There's too much use made of bold and capital letters. The repetitive listing of sections (and the use of roman numerals which, in general, are not that well understood) and the distance from the section headings to the page numbers all add up to a poor contents page. It makes the reader work too hard. Keeping the example's section headings, it would be better laid out like this:

**Contents**

| | |
|---|---|
| 1 About the home | **1** |
| 2 Summary | **2** |
| 3 Records | **3** |
| 4 The environment | **6** |
| 5 Maintenance and structural repair | **9** |

This shows that design doesn't need to be fancy, complicated or fussy to work. Quite often, the simple is more effective. The design of something should improve its readability not detract from or overpower it. The second contents page above looks better but is also easier to read. And we should content ourselves with that.

**highlighting**

In the old black and white days of Corona, ribbons and return key *chings*, the best ways to highlight text were to underline it, letter by letter, or type each letter twice for that natural additive-free emboldened look. Now that the future has arrived with its screens, toner cartridges and laser printers, typewriters are being gradually de-commissioned because they don't fit in anymore; they don't know how to crash, for a start. They are, though, useful relics for filling in forms, especially those marked 'application'.

Despite having the ability (at the push of a mouse) to put text in **bold** or *italics*, underlining has not only survived but remains a popular choice. And I don't know why. Using lines as part of the design of a page can be effective. But underlining text to highlight it is unnecessary. Indeed as shown below, underlining lower case words looks ugly as the line cuts through the tails of some letters. So let's draw a line under this once and for all.

If you want to highlight the word 'highlighting' – here are some options:

| | |
|---|---|
| **highlighting** | bold |
| *highlighting* | italics |
| ***highlighting*** | bold italic |
| highlighting | larger fontsize – useful for headings but should be avoided in body of text |
| **highlighting** | larger fontsize in bold |
| HIGHLIGHTING | capital letters – if you must |
| <u>highlighting</u> | underlining – looks ugly as it cuts through the letter 'g' and does the same to 'j', 'p', 'y' and 'q'. |
| **<u>HIGHLIGHTING</u>** | capital letters, bold, underlined, larger fontsize, the whole shebang because it's **really** important |

Remember that highlighting (whichever you choose) can only be effective if it is used sparingly. I knew one admin assistant who typed everything in bold (reflecting the importance of everything, no doubt). It was ugly, harsh and overbearing to read. On page 86 is an example that follows our general advice and on page 87 is an example that ignores it.

**using visuals**

The purpose of illustrations is to, well, illustrate: to show your point or findings in a simple, clear graphic that does the job of many words in one look. But it must be clear to be effective. Using a 3D visual graphic might look hip, young and trendy but if it's purpose isn't immediately apparent, then it's very likely that

# The importance of layout

## 1 Prefer portrait

1.1   We're simply more used to reading things with the page this way up. If you use landscape you run the very real risk of disgruntling your reader because:

- it's difficult to hold and pages are difficult to turn

- the number of words on each line will usually be far more than they're used to causing them to struggle with coping with it

- it's more easily damaged

- of its unusual format, it leaves your reader unsure about the report altogether.

1.2   However, if you are making use of charts, graphs or other essential illustrations that look uncomfortably squashed up or which lose their clarity when condensed to fit on the page, then you have little option but to call landscape off the subs bench.

## 2 Think space

2.1   Modern design has learnt the usefulness of nothing: *nothing* is good. The more nothing, the more space you can leave on a page, the better. This has a pleasing effect on the eye. If you see an uncluttered, logically laid out page your eyes tell your brain 'Hey, we can cope with this!' The easier on the eye a page is the easier it is to get to grips with what is being said.

2.2   The landscape page example is too irregular and inconsistent in design, and far too cluttered. It turns us off. The poorly thought-out design on the landscape example reflects the thinking of the arguments. This example makes use of space. The more white, the less text, the easier it is to read.

2.3   The headings, for example, have space above and below them, giving them room to breathe and helping them (as is the bold) to stand out clearly. Also the use of bullet points in 1.1 help to create space, specially as there is a free line between each point - again keeping the list uncluttered and improving its readability.

2.4   Finally, indenting the text consistently, as well as creating more space on the page also helps give the page an ordered look, which gives the reader confidence that thought, time and effort went into your report. And what is written without effort is generally read without pleasure: as somebody who had a bit of an influence on English once said.

## *ANNEXE THREE: SECTION A*   2.0 THE IMPORTANCE OF LAYOUT IN WRITING REPORTS

### 2.1 LANDSCAPE

2.1.1 Some people seem to have it in their small heads that if you lay out the occasional page in landscape it is annoying for people to have to keep turning the pages around. I think that it shows you to be the type of person always looking to try new things because you're tired of doing it the same way all the time. And anyway, if you are using graphs or charts it is sometimes impossible to fit them comfortably in portrait. What would we do then, I ask you? Exactly.

2.1.2 In short, there's no good reason not to have your paper this way around. It's real big and it's real clever. It's true. There's been documentaries and books about it and everything.

### 2.2 FONTS

2.2.1 Not the cool, leather-jacketed scourge of Jefferson High from *Happy Days* but the type of typeface you use. It's great these days because there's loads of them. My computer has got over 50 of them.

(a) You should experiment with as many as you can because:

(i) they wouldn't be there if you weren't supposed to use them

(ii) shows how creative you are

(iii) It makes your work look better and stops your reader getting bored - keeps them on their toes

### 3.0 REFERENCING
### 3.1 USES FOR REFERENCING

•It is very useful to use references. For example, the scientifically proven fact that using a variety of fonts keeps your readers on their toes can be readily accessed at: **Annexe 3, Section A, 2.2.1. (a) (iii).** Dead simple. [**NB.** Page numbers are helpful, too].

### 3.2 WHAT TO USE FOR REFERENCES

3.2.1 Most people like using numbers but you can be more creative if you want: think about using letters (EITHER CAPITAL LETTERS TO MAKE THEM STAND OUT MORE - EXCELLENT FOR SECTION HEADINGS LIKE ON THIS EXAMPLE); or lower case if they are on what I call the subs-bench: that is, if they're *sub*-sections or *sub*-points; Roman numerals are good as well because they can be in capitals as in V, IV, III, II, I Thunderbirds are GO!! Or in lower case as in i, ii testing, testing, i, ii. Put these in brackets for that extra special bit of class.

### 4.1 HIGHLIGHTING

**4.1.1.** You get highlights everywhere nowadays: Match of the Day, my mate Daryl's hair and reports. **IF YOU WANT SOMETHING TO REALLY STAND OUT BECAUSE IT IS SO IMPORTANT AND YOU NEED TO LET PEOPLE KNOW THAT, THEN YOU SHOULD GO FOR CAPITAL LETTERS THAT ARE IN BOLD AND UNDERLINED. SOME PEOPLE RECKON THAT IT IS DIFFICULT TO READ LINES OF TEXT IN CAPITAL LETTERS BUT THAT'S THEIR PROBLEM BECAUSE HOW ELSE WILL THEY KNOW JUST HOW IMPORTANT THE MESSAGE IS?** I rest my case, m'lud. End of.

the only thing it's illustrating is that you've got a software package that can do 3D graphics and you know how to use it.

The visuals shown below are examples of a table text, a bar chart, and line charts.

**Tables** present data in a way that can make it easy to understand. make sure that the data is easy to understand. It is important that the reader is able to work out quickly the information without getting muddled between rows and columns.

Make sure that you label your columns. It might be obvious to you, but your reader is not always just you, so make it obvious for other readers as well.

Highlight the point you are trying to make. If you want to emphasise a point – say it in a picture and explain it words. For example:

| Month | Day meals delivered | | | | | | | |
|---|---|---|---|---|---|---|---|---|
| | Monday | Tuesday | Wednesday | Thursday | Friday | Saturday | Sunday | Average per month |
| January | 1233 | 1292 | 1243 | 1258 | 1235 | 1345 | 1198 | 1257.4 |
| February | 1237 | 1267 | 1269 | 1267 | 1235 | 1245 | 1187 | 1243.9 |
| March | 1245 | 1301 | 1294 | 1275 | 1301 | 1297 | 1195 | 1272.6 |
| April | 1345 | 1347 | 1324 | 1335 | 1368 | 1343 | 1145 | 1315.3 |
| May | 1354 | 1370 | 1378 | 1389 | 1356 | 1389 | 1134 | 1338.6 |
| June | 1356 | 1326 | 1321 | 1342 | 1334 | 1345 | 1193 | 1316.7 |
| July | 1401 | 1336 | 1327 | 1332 | 1350 | 1345 | 1135 | 1318.0 |
| August | 890 | 840 | 856 | 804 | 837 | 833 | 1134 | 884.9 |
| September | 1325 | 1343 | 1326 | 1367 | 1342 | 1356 | 1167 | 1318.0 |
| October | 1367 | 1369 | 1374 | 1395 | 1386 | 1345 | 1156 | 1341.7 |
| November | 1401 | 1395 | 1403 | 1423 | 1378 | 1398 | 1134 | 1361.7 |
| December | 1472 | 1459 | 1463 | 1448 | 1484 | 1435 | 1175 | 1419.4 |
| Total meals delivered 1997 | | | | | | | | |

As you can see, from *figure 1* above, deliveries of meals are much lower in August. This is because of the number of holidays taken by customers during this month.

There are a number of types of charts you could use to illustrate the same point as above. But you should remember the type of information you are trying to put across and choose one that best illustrates this. The following **bar chart** shows quite effectively where the dip in meals delivered occurs:

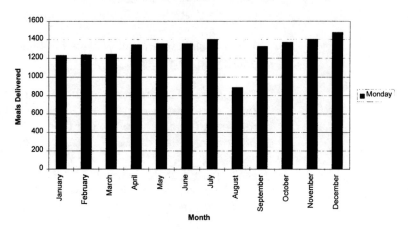

Meals delivered in 1997 by Highfield City Council : Monday

However, you could present the same information on a **line chart** and the result is an even clearer illustration of how dramatically deliveries are affected in August:

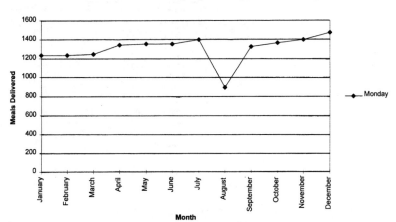

Meals delivered in 1997 by Highfield City Council : Monday

And remember that you can move the start point on the axes to either improve the presentation or make the impact of the chart more dramatic. For example, the above line chart starts its vertical axis (the numbers of meals delivered) at 200 and rises by 200 each time. The following example, however, starts at 700 and rises by 100 each time. The effect is, as you can see, far more dramatic:

**Meals delivered in 1997 by Highfield City Council : Monday**

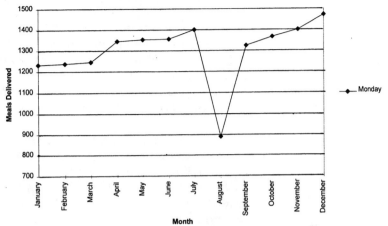

One final point: if you are able to do so, think about using colour on a chart as this can improve your presentation even further. The example below shows that, if used in black and white, despite our best efforts it's very difficult to work out any of the detail, although the general trend can be picked out.

Number of meals delivered to residents in 1997 by Highfield City Council

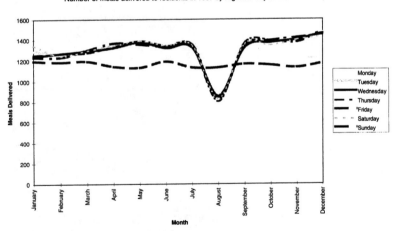

***watermarks***

People enjoy playing and experimenting with their computers. Quite right, too. What people do in the privacy of their own home is largely their own affair. Trouble is too often they want us all to know it. So they subject their work (and us) to the latest gimmick they've either come across or gained their gold proficiency medal for. The watermark is one such gimmick. It might look good but it just gets in the way.

Proper watermarks are those that you can only see when you hold them up to light. However, the watermarks at our disposal are less sophisticated. They are placed in the background as if stamped on the page; the text is then printed over them. At best it detracts from your report, at worst it blocks out text and makes reading a chore. Whenever I've come across a watermark it has been used overwhelmingly to say 'draft report', 'confidential' or some such similar sentiment. As in the example below, from a Social Services Quality Assurance Division.

However, many organisations swear by them. It makes it crystal clear, they say, for example, that a report is **not** for public consumption. This may be true but you could get the same effect by having such a direction printed at the top of each page – that way, the text isn't obstructed. Watermarks like the example given dampen your reader's interest. Wash your hands of them.

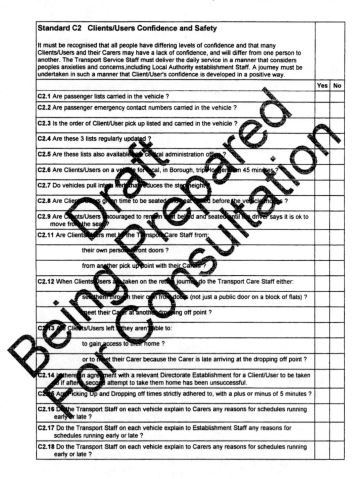

| Standard C2  Clients/Users Confidence and Safety | Yes | No |
|---|---|---|
| It must be recognised that all people have differing levels of confidence and that many Clients/Users and their Carers may have a lack of confidence, and will differ from one person to another. The Transport Service Staff must deliver the daily service in a manner that considers peoples anxieties and concerns, including Local Authority establishment Staff. A journey must be undertaken in such a manner that Client/User's confidence is developed in a positive way. | | |
| C2.1 Are passenger lists carried in the vehicle ? | | |
| C2.2 Are passenger emergency contact numbers carried in the vehicle ? | | |
| C2.3 Is the order of Client/User pick up listed and carried in the vehicle ? | | |
| C2.4 Are these 3 lists regularly updated ? | | |
| C2.5 Are these lists also available to Central administration office ? | | |
| C2.6 Are Clients/Users on a vehicle for local, in Borough, trips longer than 45 minutes ? | | |
| C2.7 Do vehicles pull into kerb that reduces the step height ? | | |
| C2.8 Are Clients/Users given time to be seated and seat belted before the vehicle moves ? | | |
| C2.9 Are Clients/Users encouraged to remain seat belted and seated until the driver says it is ok to move from the seat? | | |
| C2.11 Are Clients/Users met by the Transport Care Staff from: | | |
| their own personal front doors ? | | |
| from another pick up point with their Carers ? | | |
| C2.12 When Clients/Users are taken on the return journey do the Transport Care Staff either: | | |
| see them through their own front doors (not just a public door on a block of flats) ? | | |
| meet their Carer at another dropping off point ? | | |
| C2.13 Are Clients/Users left if they aren't able to: | | |
| to gain access to their home ? | | |
| or to meet their Carer because the Carer is late arriving at the dropping off point ? | | |
| C2.14 Is there an agreement with a relevant Directorate Establishment for a Client/User to be taken to if after a second attempt to take them home has been unsuccessful. | | |
| C2.15 Are Picking Up and Dropping off times strictly adhered to, with a plus or minus of 5 minutes ? | | |
| C2.16 Do the Transport Staff on each vehicle explain to Carers any reasons for schedules running early or late ? | | |
| C2.17 Do the Transport Staff on each vehicle explain to Establishment Staff any reasons for schedules running early or late ? | | |
| C2.18 Do the Transport Staff on each vehicle explain to Carers any reasons for schedules running early or late ? | | |

# Letters

Some of the guidelines given above for laying out reports will, of course, be relevant for letter writing (use of space, highlighting and so on). In this section, we will show an example of a made-up letter and highlight areas for you to think about.

1 Address of sender

2 Telephone and other numbers

3 Date

4 Other information

5 References

6 Address of recipient

7 Greeting

8 Heading

9 Body of letter

10 Ending

11 Signature of sender

12 Name of sender

13 Title of sender

14 Enclosures

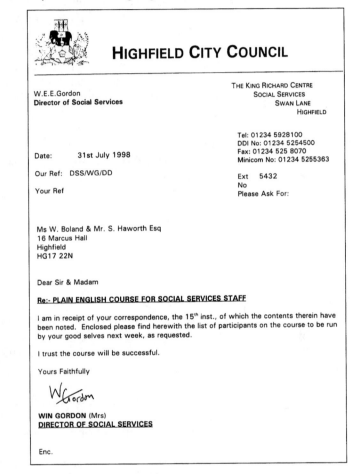

## HIGHFIELD CITY COUNCIL

W.E.E.Gordon
**Director of Social Services**

THE KING RICHARD CENTRE
SOCIAL SERVICES
SWAN LANE
HIGHFIELD

Date:     31st July 1998

Our Ref:   DSS/WG/DD

Your Ref

Tel: 01234 5928100
DDI No: 01234 5254500
Fax: 01234 525 8070
Minicom No: 01234 5255363

Ext    5432
No
Please Ask For:

Ms W. Boland & Mr. S. Haworth Esq
16 Marcus Hall
Highfield
HG17 22N

Dear Sir & Madam

Re:- PLAIN ENGLISH COURSE FOR SOCIAL SERVICES STAFF

I am in receipt of your correspondence, the 15th inst., of which the contents therein have been noted. Enclosed please find herewith the list of participants on the course to be run by your good selves next week, as requested.

I trust the course will be successful.

Yours Faithfully

*W Gordon*

**WIN GORDON** (Mrs)
**DIRECTOR OF SOCIAL SERVICES**

Enc.

**let's get it letter perfect**

*1 Address*

Modern convention has the address set out straight and punctuation free. This sloping address is unusual in official letters. Quite often, depending on the style adopted for the organisation's logo, you will see addresses laid out in a straight line across the top or bottom of the letter. Again, if this is the case, the address will usually be punctuation-free. Also prefer to use lower case letters as they help readability. We should not have to suffer capital punishment and, except for the first letter of each word, all capital letters should be guillotined in favour of the lower-cases.

**2 Telephone and other numbers**

This is poorly laid out and labelled. Where possible, abbreviations (Tel, DDI, No) should be avoided. Sometimes symbols (☎ ✉ ✏) can be helpful. If possible, prefer *phone number* or *phone*, *fax number* or *fax* and so on. The printing of two phone numbers on our example is confusing and, more so, given that the extension number is isolated from the phone number it relates to. The use of *DDI* (direct dialling) is pompous techno-speak. The use of *direct line* would be more helpful. Readability would also be helped if the numbers were broken up into three parts (the use of brackets for the prefix (01234) is helpful to the reader) – the prefix and a division in the number. Six digit numbers should be split three-three – 456 987 – and seven digit numbers should be divided into three-four – 234 9876.

**3 Date**

Even something as simple as the date cannot find universal acceptance about how it should be laid out. It's all a matter of style and taste. You can order a date in any of the following ways (leaving out the day):

| | | |
|---|---|---|
| 31 July 1934 | 31st. July, 1934 | July, 31st., 1934 |
| 31st July 1934 | 31st July 1934 | 31/7/1934 |
| 31st., July, 1934 | 31-7-1934 | July, 31st 1934 |
| 31, July, 1934 | July 31 1934 | July, 31st. 1934 |
| 31st July, 1934 | July 31st 1934 | July 31st 1934 |

And all of these again but replacing *1934* with just *34*.

I prefer the first example. This punctuation-free date reads better, looks cleaner and is less fussy. Also by preferring the *31 July 1934* construction, you don't need to mentally convert the date, and as the numbers are divided by letters it gives us a pleasant symmetry. Your organisation may, of course, have a house style for dates which you will be expected to follow.

**4 Other information**

In our example, this section is laid out clumsily. The extension number is adrift from the relevant phone number. The use of abbreviations (*Ext* and *No*) are made even more confusing by being on different lines. The *Please Ask For:* is useful for senior people who have been forced to (usually) reply to someone but do not want anything more to do with them – instructing the recipient to deal with an underling in future. This is used a lot in organisations where letters go out in the name of one person (usually the power-crazed) rather than the poor writer's own name. So people like Mr Nilsson, say, have to write letters in the third person and end up writing ridiculous things like 'please contact my colleague Mr Nilsson who would be happy to discuss this further with you'. If someone is trusted to write a letter then they should take responsibility for it, write it in the first person and sign it for themselves.

## 5 References

Our ref, your ref, their ref, whose ref, come on ref, why ref? Taking a random sample of this week's post, I note that, with the exception of those nice people from the tax office, nobody uses the *Our Ref* for anything other than the initials of the person who has written it (and who signs it in any case) and presumably the initials of the person typing the letter. Still, it persists as a convention. If your organisation keeps records that are filed (manually or electronically) by a reference number, then the our ref/your ref is indispensable. If not, then it is entirely dispensable.

## 6 Address of recipient

This is particularly useful if you are sending a letter to someone at their work address. Quite often, organisations have a central post room that opens all letters and then distributes them. Having the person's name on the letter helps make sure that it gets to the right person. The address can also be typed on the letter so that when it is folded the address fits neatly into the window of an envelope. However, I have yet to work for an organisation that's actually cracked this. It seems that only advanced training in origami can prepare someone for the ordeal of making the address fit the window.

A difficult area, at times, can be how to address someone. A formal letter or your organisation's house style may require a formal title for recipients. For men, an uncomplicated *Mr* (without the full stop – I think we all know that it's short for *Mister* now) suffices. For women, we have three possibilities: *Mrs, Miss* and *Ms*. Men, unlike women, have never had to worry about distinguishing whether they are married or not. Potential liberation from prying into women's private lives began in 1950s America with the introduction of *Ms* (pronounced *muzz* or *mizz*). It arrived in the UK in the 1960s. However, the Passport Office only officially accepted it as a title in 1974. To deny its existence or to refuse its acceptance is an old fashioned, sexist and class-ridden anomaly. Why are my thoughts suddenly drawn to south-west London, and strawberries and cream? Anyone for tennis?

Nowadays, *Ms* is afforded full word status in dictionaries. For example, *Collins* defines it as a 'title used before the name of a woman to avoid indicating whether she is married or not'. However, there is no entry in my *Shorter Oxford English Dictionary* (1992 version). Although, interestingly, it points out that *Mrs* used to be applied to single women as it stood for *Mistress*.

The guide has to be: give people the title they give themselves. If they call themselves *Miss* you should respect their preference. Some women actually dislike *Ms* because they feel it represents a radical feminism with which they have no truck. However, if you are not aware of a woman's preference (and you *have* to give her a title) then the safest option is *Ms*. But only if you're sure that your addressee *is* a woman. Names like Nicky, Bernie, Chris, Kim, and so on are as likely to be male names as female. So, exercise caution. The only thing worse than getting someone's gender wrong is spelling their name wrong. The clue should be to see how they sign themselves off at the end of a letter. If they sign it 'Sammy Shilton', then a good guide is to address your letter as such and reply to 'Dear Sammy Shilton' or 'Dear Sammy' dependent on the perceived formality of the letter. It may be inelegant to some, but it's how that person likes to be known.

We will only deal with commoners or gardeners' titles and not those of rank or nobility. I recognise this may be a flaw for those people living or working in the home counties or parts of London well west of Canning Town. These are people, who include the Cambridgeshire councillor who asked: 'Does the Children Act apply in Fenland?'; or the health authority inspector who remarked: 'We certainly don't need plain English. This is East Surrey, after all, dear. Thank you.'

*The Complete Letter Writer for Gentlemen* kindly informed us that there is 'precise instruction as to the forms to be observed in addressing people of standing, a matter for which even socially expert people sometimes display ignorance'. Clearly, *The Write Stuff* believes that ignorance is bliss. Apparently we're *supposed* to address a bishop as 'The Rt. Rev. The Lord Bishop of ___'. And not *Dear Bish*. I'm not even sure where ___ is, anyway. If someone was a 'person of standing' (translation = officer) in the Royal Navy, you are supposed to put RN after their name. Why? Do we write Pip Roberts SSD? I think not. Surprisingly, *Debrett's Peerage & Baronetage* or *Correct Form* do not figure in my bibliography. Rather laudable, I thought.

The use of the anachronistic *Esq* is fading but still crops up. It is an abbreviation for *esquire*. An esquire, in medieval times, was 'a young man of gentle birth' (*Oxford English Dictionary*) – an attendant to a knight, carrying his shield and, ahem, rendering other services as required (but the less said about that, the better). Later on, esquire became a title of rank with increasing numbers laying claim to it (sons of peers, judges, barristers as well as indicating property ownership). By the mid 20th century, it had lost all significance of rank and became a courtesy title for all men. However, convention dictated that it could not be used unless you knew the name or initials of the man, or if you used any other title (such as *Mr*, *Capt* and so on): *Richard Shaw, Esq.* being correct, but *Mr Liam Daish, Esq.* not so. However, as far as we're concerned it's an unnecessary formality – so I'd avoid it if I was you, squire.

## 7 Greeting

Sometimes known as the *salutation* or *superscription*, the plain old greeting, in much the ways talked about above, also causes unnecessary grief at times. If you know the person you are writing to, a friendly and informal *Dear Noel* is acceptable. If you do not know the person you are writing to (but are confident of their title) a formal *Dear Mr Whelan* is appropriate. Or, if you're playing it safe, a *Dear Noel Whelan* is best. And certainly preferable to the impersonal and unthinking banality of *Dear Sir/Madam*. If you know the person's name, you should always include that (in whatever form you choose) in the greeting and try to avoid a bland and over-formal *Dear Sir* or *Dear Madam*.

Finally, if you are looking for the ultimate in the human or personal touch, you could consider handwriting the greeting. I favour this approach as it confirms to the recipient that you have taken the time to respond to them personally. If you take this approach, it's best to use a blue ink as black ink could simply look photocopied, and do likewise when signing the letter.

## 8 Heading

Headings are useful. They help the reader to find out quickly what the letter is about. This means the heading should be clear, specific and to the point. Headings should be either left-aligned or (preferably) centred. They should be positioned between the greeting and the main body of the report.

Headings all too often are set out in capital letters, in bold and underlined to show just how jolly important they are. Capital letters should be avoided as, in headings of over three words, they start to shout at you (which is very bad manners) and become rather threatening. Prefer lowercase, where possible. As the heading is at the top of the page, the only highlighting it needs is bold. This sets it off from the rest of the letter (provided you have followed *The Write Stuff*'s advice and used bold sparingly elsewhere). The underlining is as unnecessary as the use of *Re:-*

No other headings use *Re:-*, so why should letters be different? It adds nothing to the meaning. *Re* doesn't actually mean 'with reference to' or 'about' (even though that is how – if at all – it is understood); it is short for *res* which is Latin for 'thing, affair, circumstance'. It gets used mostly in – shock, horror – legal documents (*In re Rex v. Whelan*). The curious punctuation mark (:-) that often follows is actually *two* punctuation marks – a colon and a dash. One or the other will suffice. That is, if you intend keeping the *Re* for old time's sake or for some such fanciful notion. But you should really put it out of its misery. It's the only sensible thing to do.

## 9 Body of the letter

We've covered this section in Chapter 4 *Structure*. However, just a couple of other points. First, the use of *inst.* is incredibly old-fashioned. Meaning 'the present month' it should be avoided, as should its cousins: *ult.* ('last month') and *prox.* ('next month'). Indeed, K G Thomson in *The Handbook of Letter Writing*, commented that inst., ult. and prox. had 'largely died out but are still used by some old-fashioned people'. And that was in 1961.

Second, the language of our made-up letter is out of place as the closing overs of the 20th century are bowled. Don't get caught out – keep your writing fresh, lively, direct and just outside the off-stump. I received a letter from someone who made over-humble use of 'your good self' and 'I beg your leave to differ' (I refused him leave, naturally). I thought the writer was going to beseech me to join the crusades at one point. This style of language is out of time and should be avoided. The 'I have the honour to be, your most obedient servant' is taking the humility of working in the public service a bridge too far.

However, below is proof that it still happens – even under new Labour. This was sent from the office of John Prescott in 1998, recommending planning permission:

RECOMMENDATION

20.    I recommend that the appeal be allowed and that listed building consent be granted subject to a standard time condition and the limitations set out in paragraph 19 above.

I have the honour to be

Sir
Your obedient Servant

P D WILSON   DipArch DipTP RIBA MRTPI
Inspector

## 10 Ending

Sometimes called the *subscription*, the ending to letters is less complicated than it used to be. It is considered that 'correct' endings depend on the greeting.

| **Greeting** | **Ending** |
|---|---|
| Dear Sir/Madam, Dear Sir, Dear Madam | *Yours faithfully* |
| Dear Mr McAllister, Dear Ms McAllister, Dear Mrs McAllister, Dear Miss McAllister | *Yours sincerely* |

We rarely see endings likes *yours truly, yours very truly* and so on anymore. Indeed, *yours faithfully* is being increasingly replaced with *yours sincerely*. The distinctions have little importance these days. I prefer the more human and friendly *Best wishes* on all letters unless the subject matter makes that inappropriate, in which case *Yours sincerely* is drafted in.

Quite often I come across letters that have ended with a typed *Yours sincerely*, but which are hand-signed *Best wishes* with the person's name. Also, there are those who type in a *With my very best wishes* but then follow it with a typed *Yours sincerely*. Now all of this smacks of the best-of-both-worlds syndrome. And it's none the worse for it, either.

Note that only the first word of your ending needs a capital letter (*Yours sincerely* and not *Yours Sincerely*). Also that the ending is punctuation-free.

It's also worth noting that *Thanks* or *Thank you* are popular sign-offs for e-mails and memos.

## 11 Signature of sender

Wherever possible you should sign your own letter. The use of stamps for efficiency rather than for necessity (where your disability prevents you making your mark) is merely the triumph of the slap of bureaucracy over the human touch. Signing your own letters shows that you can be bothered, that you care. If you are unable to sign personally, and your letter needs to go out before you can be back to sign it, then get someone to sign it on your behalf.

If you do get someone to sign a letter for you, and you prefer the *pp* method, make sure they sign their own name and not yours. The Latin *pp* stands for *per procurationem* which means 'by the agency of the other'. This means that the pp should go before the name of the person signing it. However, avoid all this unnecessary complication, and get someone to sign it (where your signature would go) adding a simple, English *for* before your typed-out name. Life is simply too short to write *for and on behalf of*.

Yours sincerely

*Gordon Milne*

P.P.**GORDON MILNE**
MANAGER

x

Yours sincerely

PP *Kirstie Maguire*

**GORDON MILNE**
MANAGER

✓

Yours sincerely

*Kirstie Maguire*

for **Gordon Strachan**
Quality Manager

✓✓

## 12 Name of sender

If your signature is anything like mine, there's no need to say why typing out your name is essential. It is purely a matter of style whether you want to put a title in (Mr, Ms, Mrs, Miss) either before your name or after it (usually in brackets). However, that is very formal. If that's your wish or aim – then carry on. If not, prefer a friendly first and last name approach.

Yours sincerely

*P A Roberts (Mrs)*

P.A. ROBERTS, BA (Hons) (MRS)
**SENIOR SOCIAL WORKER**

x

Yours sincerely

*Pip Roberts*

**Pip Roberts**
Senior Social Worker

✓

## 13 Title

A title is not essential, but gives the reader an idea of who or what you are – just in case your letter hasn't already done that for them. It can also give you a sense of importance (if you have a suitably grand title) or a sense of despair and helplessness (if yours includes words like *junior, assistant* or *dogsbody*).

If you do have a grand title, try to avoid elaborating it further by sticking it in bold and capital letters. You've probably worked hard for your title but try to keep it in the background and out of your reader's face. If you do have a pompous or overlong title (and these days they are about as rare as a referral) do what an increasing number of people do – and make up a shorter one. I once had the official job title of *Inspection and Quality Assurance Manager*. I changed it to *Inspection Manager*. Nobody noticed. Or cared.

## 14 Enclosures

Usually abbreviated to *Enc.,* this is used to indicate that certain items (sometimes listed) are enclosed with the letter. Also used as a handy reminder for the typist to actually enclose the items or (probably more likely) ask you for them. Rather than use *Enc* or *Enclosures,* prefer to type out a fuller, clearer and more friendly *Please find enclosed* and list the items that are, indeed, enclosed. You hope.

Here's how that letter might now look:

**HIGHFIELD CITY COUNCIL**

W.E.E.Gordon
**Director of Social Services**

KING RICHARD CENTRE
SOCIAL SERVICES
SWAN LANE
HIGHFIELD

**Date:** 31 July 1998

**Our Ref:** DSS/WG/DD

**Your Ref:**

**Phone:** (01234) 525 4500

**Fax:** (01234) 525 8070

**Minicom:** (01234) 525 5363

Wilma Boland & Simon Haworth
16 Marcus Hall
Highfield
HG17 22N

*Dear Wilma & Simon*

**Plain English for Social Services Training Course**

Thank you for your letter dated 28 July 1998. Please find enclosed, as requested, a list of all the staff who will be attending your course next week. If there's anything else you need, please feel free to call me.

I look forward to meeting you next week.

Yours sincerely

*W Gordon*

**Win Gordon**
Director of Social Services

Please find enclosed: *list of course participants*

## our customer care report

Following on from chapter 4 *Structure*, where we decided on the structure of the report, we now need to think about the layout. Our report structure is straightforward, so our layout will be too. But we need to think about how the layout can strengthen our message. Our report is an update but it's real purpose is to try and put *customer care* back into the limelight.

We should aim for a simple design but with something to attract people to our message. The largest section will be section 4 *Where we are now*. So, perhaps we could concentrate on helping to make this stand out. As we are trying to promote customer care perhaps we could look for a device that highlights good practice examples. We could make use of 'good example' boxes that are set in the text that could draw attention to the good work around at the moment. This will help focus readers' minds on what can be achieved if, as our report will suggest, there is better co-ordination and management of customer care. It will also help to deflect potential criticism from councillors that little has been done to carry out the department's policy.

The example boxes will also help to break up text and add to the overall look and readability of the report. A simple but effective design could be:

| **Good Practice** | *Social Services* |
|---|---|
| | The Social Services Inspection Unit held a seminar for regulated service providers to discover what they thought about the purpose, principles and methods of inspection. It was very well attended by 88 people. The outcome of the seminar was a policy document which will be entitled *An Inspector Calls* that will set down clear standards for service providers to judge the service provided by the inspection unit and its inspectors. |

Used throughout the text, this should look good.

# Editing

# Chapter 9 – Editing

*'I have made this [letter] longer than usual, only because I have not had the time to make it shorter'*

Blaise Pascal

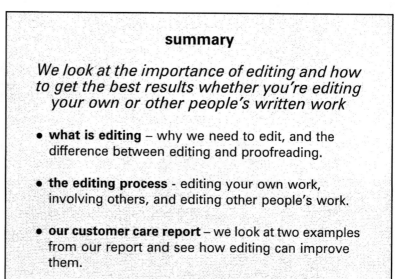

**summary**

*We look at the importance of editing and how to get the best results whether you're editing your own or other people's written work*

- **what is editing** – why we need to edit, and the difference between editing and proofreading.

- **the editing process** - editing your own work, involving others, and editing other people's work.

- **our customer care report** – we look at two examples from our report and see how editing can improve them.

## introduction

*'A writer is unfair to himself when he is unable to be hard on himself'*
*Marianne Moore*

The three most important things you can do to improve your work is to edit, edit and edit. Editing all your written work (including short letters or memos) is important. Remember that almost everything you write, even the shortest memo, could probably be improved with revision. Very little is ever spot on first time around. For longer pieces of work, such as reports, then editing is essential. And think of it as essential. Don't think of editing as an admittance of failure. It is a positive aspect of the whole writing process. Every good writer edits their work. You're checking for accuracy, clarity and whether you have met your brief as well as possible. You are fine-tuning your piece of work.

We will concentrate our discussion in this chapter on the methods, tools and outcomes of editing reports. But, as ever, the principles can be adopted and refined for editing any piece of work.

Editing is your chance to check (as objectively as you can) that you've said what you wanted to say in the best way possible. Have you made everything easy for the reader?

It is worth noting the difference between *proof-reading* (or *proofing*) your report and *editing* it. If you are proofing, you are looking for accuracy of:

- spelling
- punctuation
- grammar

Whereas if you are editing you are making judgements about the clarity of your writing and as a result may edit out or re-write parts of your report. Of course, you can do both at the same time but it's always wise to have a read through for proofing purposes only. This allows you to concentrate on each word in isolation, making it more likely for you to spot mistakes.

You can edit your own work as you go along and, crucially, when you have finished writing the whole thing. Editing at the end is important as you get to read through the whole piece of work. This gives you a sense of how the whole thing sounds and works. Is there a continuity of argument, style and format? Is there any unnecessary repetition? Does it do its intended job? Are there any spelling, punctuation, grammar or typing mistakes? Is there any redundant repetition? Is it clear, accurate and convincing? Is there any needless repetition?

## the editing process

**introduction**

If time permits (and you should always try to seek permission) you should leave your report alone. Lock it away and give the key to someone you don't like. Forget it. Deny its existence. It is no report of yours. The longer you can leave it, the better.

This means that when you return to it for editing you are almost seeing it for the first time. This is very important as the two most useless people in the western hemisphere to edit or proof your work are Cleopatra and you. Cleopatra because she died over 2000 years ago (and would probably need to ask her mummy, anyway) and you because you know what's coming and don't see what's really there.

'All good writers rewrite. They do not expect to get it right first time. They only expect to get it on paper first time'

*David G Lyon*

With your mind and eyes afresh, it is remarkable the number of things you will undoubtedly notice. There will be mistakes, clumsy and confusing sentences, pompous words and jargon –

guaranteed or your money back. There are three aspects of editing that we will look at. These are:

- editing your own work
- involving others
- editing someone else's work

**doing it yourself**

Once again, there's no right or wrong way of doing this. It's more a question of what you prefer or what works best for you. There are two ways of editing:

- on the screen
- on paper

**on the screen**

If you do your own typing, there is something gratifying about creating your work on the screen. Except when the screen turns into a scream when the computer crashes (again). But you are in control and not at the mercy of your typist who, as experience savagely recalls, will probably only treat your written comments on drafts as rough guidance.

**Editing on the screen**

| *good points* | *bad points* |
|---|---|
| • saves time – changes can be made immediately | • you lose the original if you type over changes and are unable to compare (or else you need to take a hard copy or save original on file) |
| • you're in control – there can't be any misunderstandings about the changes (if you need to use a typist, which can also introduce new mistakes) | • you can't see 'the whole' but can only work through section by section |

**editing on paper**

With all the advantages of working on screen, many people (me included) do like (at least occasionally) to write in longhand and (almost always) to edit in longhand. I tend to work on the screen and then edit in longhand from a printed copy, known as a *hard copy*. On reports and longer pieces of work, I find it best to print a draft with the lines double-spaced. This means that I have room between lines for rewriting, making notes and other assorted variety packs of fun-size scribblings.

'The waste-paper basket is the writer's best friend'
*Issac Bashevis Singer*

Once I'm happy with my handwritten changes, I then try to leave the project once again as long as possible. This is not always possible, I know, but if time is kind, take advantage. This means that when I go to put the changes on screen, I'm testing those changes again, analysing their effectiveness. It's a form of secondary editing.

If you are editing your work, it means that you can be as honest and as brutal as you dare with your red pen (or your choice of the season's must-have shades of ink). The only feelings you can hurt are your own.

Some people prefer to go through a draft two, three or more times, each time with a different coloured pen. This serves three purposes: first, the more you edit, the better your chances of improving your work. Second, the use of colours readily (or blue-edly or green-edly) show the number of changes made in each editing stage; this is helpful because you can, over time, build up an understanding of the effectiveness of each stage. And third, there may be a number of changes to make, but, hey, look how colourful it is. It could be brighten up the coldest day.

### Editing by long-hand

| *good points* | *bad points* |
| --- | --- |
| • you have a record of the original | • takes longer, could lead to 'wasted' paper |
| • you can judge the change against the original | • typist can misunderstand or can't read your handwritten changes – adding time to the process |
| • you can leave marks to come back and check or use other visual aids | |
| • it's 'easier' to see the whole report as the reaer may well see it | |

**involving others**

As you are the *undisputed world champion worst proof-reader of your own work in the history of the universe ever*, it is a good idea to let someone (whose opinions you value and trust) have a look. Even if you have come back to your report fresh, you may still miss things that are only manifestly obvious when pointed out.

I remember sending the first finished draft of *Plain English for Social Services* to seven people for comments. I had proof-read the draft twice. When the comments came back, all of them had spotted mistakes that I had missed, and all of them spotted mistakes that each other missed. While adding in the corrections, I came across even more mistakes that we all had missed. Finally, when the final draft went to a professional proof-reader, even more mistakes were picked out. And all these mistakes found in a book on the use of English. It's a cold, bad, unforgiving old world out there, and you need all the help you can get.

Having people comment on a draft has two potentially good outcomes. First, you have a new pair of eyes look over what you've written. This is helpful not only for picking out mistakes in the text but also to comment on the readability, accuracy and soundness of the report as a whole. Second, it helps build relationships with people. They feel valued that you would welcome what they have to say and, as a result, dedicate care and attention to your draft. They may also return the compliment with their work.

'Blot out, correct, insert, refine/Enlarge, diminish, interline'
*Jonathan Swift*

If someone does read a draft for you, a short note of thanks is a good policy. Particularly if you tell them which bits you have changed as a result of their comments. This is not only a common courtesy but also makes the person feel valued. And, again, will encourage them to do the same job again next time, with perhaps even more precision as they realise that you actually do take notice of what they say.

Also, you shouldn't always delay sending out a draft for comment if you're not happy with it. Sometimes you just know that there's something awkward, not right or confusing about a section of the report. It might be something that you just can't seem to organise or put right. Be honest. Tell people that you feel unhappy about a section and you would particularly welcome comments on that part, and suggestions for improving it. This might be hard for you to do. You may feel too proud or worried that people will be judging not only your work but *you* as well. Or, worse still, you might feel inadequate because, somehow, you feel you are not doing your job properly. Try to feel more positive about yourself and your work. A little help can go a long way.

## re-editing

Remember that while editing can help improve your written work, you will have to stop at some stage. There is a danger that you can edit the life out of your work. Strike a balance that allows excellence and time to compromise with each other without losing face.

## editing other people's work

If you manage people or have responsibility for their written work on a specific project, you may need to review and edit their work. The way or the style you choose to do this can, at times, be more important than what you do. Your style should encourage staff to write well and you should always check other people's work as constructively as possible.

The personal and working relationship between writer and editor needs to be healthy for this process to be positive and productive. If there is a personality clash, this could lead to a volatile situation which could descend easily into a destructive rather than constructive exercise. When it comes to involving others, good relationships are the key to successful editing and revision.

This means trying to avoid giving a piece of work the red pen treatment that makes the writer feel that Miss or Sir has marked their essay 'two out of ten' or dismissed it with a D minus. It's not the use of red ink, necessarily, that causes the grief, as you do need an alternatively coloured pen to help your comments and changes stand out. It's the manner of its use: is it used constructively or destructively?

'The business of selection and revision is simply hell for me – my efforts to cut out 50,000 words may sometimes result in my adding 75,000'
*Thomas Wolfe*

One senior health authority manager once told me that she never uses a red pen *when* (not *if*, note) she corrects written work because of the bad public image of red (the colour of danger, final bill demands and the occasional Manchester United shirt). So, her remedy to blitz a page with pink or light purple ink is missing the point. A sea of any colour, no matter how soft, can be a hard knock to the confidence of a writer.

People *can* (as I contend) generally lack confidence in their writing. This means that a piece of work is handed in with a degree of trepidation at the best of times. If it is flung back with rivers of red ink flowing through it, with sentence after sentence struck out, what little confidence the writer may have had will be damaged, perhaps never to be repaired. It might be better to suggest that the writer looks again at certain parts of a report and explain why, rather than re-writing their work wholesale.

Sit down with the writer and go through your comments and points with them (try to avoid words like 'corrections' even for spelling or typing mistakes), so they are clear about what you're trying to say and why. This should be done in an open, helpful and constructive way. Sit so you can both see the report at the same time. Allow the writer to explain why they did something that you feel doesn't work. Talk through the arguments. This also gives the writer a chance to disagree with you and feel able to do so and say why. Top manager as you are, they just might have a point. Once you have gone through the report, if the writer understands (and, hopefully, agrees with) your view, they can go away and rewrite it for themselves. This encourages them to use their words and protects their sense of ownership of the work.

It also makes very good sense to help improve the writing skills of your staff as this will reduce the time you have to spend editing their work.

**things to check for**

When editing other people's work, you should check for three things:

- check the overall piece of work
- check it meets the brief
- check the detail

### check the overall piece of work

Before you start dotting the j's and crossing the f's, it's always useful (and respectful) to read through the whole report. You can look at the report and get a sense of:

- the structure
- the tone and style
- the flow of ideas and argument
- how it looks

With a sense of the whole, this can help you decide where the fine-tuning needs to take place. It's helpful to start with the big picture before you focus on the detail of each brush stroke.

### check the brief

With a sense of the whole, judge how successful the report has been in meeting the brief. This means checking how the report:

- meets the purpose
- achieves its intended outcome
- meets the needs of the target audience

### check the detail

How you judge the report's effectiveness overall helps narrow your focus on the detail. For example, does it come across as too wordy and pompous? Then pick out the big words, gobbledygook and jargon. Is there too much text on the page? Then pick out paragraphs that can be split up and shortened to create space. And so on.

In examining the detail, check:

- spelling and typing (you would have to question the bedtime reading of the typist who typed *throb* for *through*, but it's happened)
- punctuation (the catastrophe that is the apostrophe *s* is always worth checking)
- grammar

- for unnecessary repetition
- word choice
- style (it might need revision for being too formal or too informal)
- that each section (summary, introduction and so on) is relevant and has all essential information
- for unnecessary detail

## our customer care report

To illustrate the editing process, we'll take a look at a couple of examples from our customer care report: a paragraph from the summary; and a good example box – as printed on page 101.

Both examples are given in the original draft form of double-spacing with handwritten notes, and are followed by the finalised typed version.

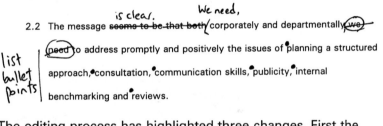

2.2 The message ~~seems to be that both~~ *is clear. We need,* corporately and departmentally ~~(we)~~ need to address promptly and positively the issues of planning a structured approach, consultation, communication skills, publicity, internal benchmarking and reviews.

*list bullet points*

The editing process has highlighted three changes. First the woolly, non-committal phrase 'seems to be' has been replaced by the shorter, sharper and more confident 'is clear' and ended the sentence there. This adds confidence, precision and assurance to our voice. Our voice now says we're confident about our findings because our method and analysis are sound.

Second, we have scratched the unnecessary word 'both'.

And third, we have preferred to put the 'issues' into a vertical list – to help each one stand out, and to aid readability. We now have:

2.2 The message is clear. We need, corporately and departmentally, to address promptly and positively the issues of:
- planning a structured approach
- consultation
- communication skills
- publicity
- internal benchmarking
- reviews.

---

| Good Practice | |
|---|---|
| | *Social Services* |

*(attended by 88 people)*

The ~~Social Services~~ Inspection Unit held a seminar for

*find out*    *Service providers*

~~regulated service providers~~ to ~~discover~~ what ~~they~~ thought

about the purpose, principles and methods of inspection. ~~It~~

~~was very well attended by 88 people~~. The outcome of the

*informed*

seminar ~~was~~ a policy document ~~which will be entitled~~ *An*

*sets*

*Inspector Calls* that ~~will set down~~ clear standards for ~~service~~

providers to judge the service provided by the inspection unit

~~and its inspectors~~.

---

Editing the above example we have, as with the first example, picked out three things. First the opening sentence has been recast. It is now concise and readable.

Second, we have made clear that the outcome of the seminar had an *influence* on the policy document rather than causing it to happen.

And third, the final phrase has been scratched as unnecessary.

---

| Good Practice | |
|---|---|
| | *Social Services* |
| | The Inspection Unit held a seminar (attended by 88 people) to find out what service providers thought about the purpose, principles and methods of inspection. The outcome of the seminar informed a policy document *An Inspector Calls* that sets clear standards for providers to judge the service provided by our inspection unit. |

We now have:

# Example report

# Chapter 10 – Example report

*'You don't say "I've done it!" You come, with a kind of horrible desperation, to realize that this will do'*

Anthony Burgess

We have taken our customer care report through all the stages. It's now time to deliver the final draft.

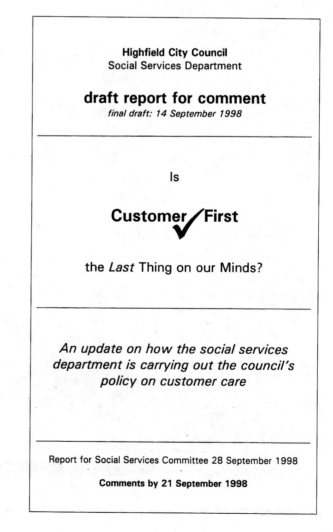

**Highfield City Council**
Social Services Department

## draft report for comment
*final draft: 14 September 1998*

Is

## Customer ✓ First

the *Last* Thing on our Minds?

*An update on how the social services department is carrying out the council's policy on customer care*

Report for Social Services Committee 28 September 1998

**Comments by 21 September 1998**

# Is **Customer First** the last thing on our minds?

*An update on how the social services department is carrying out the council's policy on customer care*

## 1    Summary

1.1    This report looks at how the department is looking to carry out the council's policy on customer care.  Based on the information received it was clear that a lot of good initiatives are either happening or are in hand.  However, these seem to be happening in isolation and are largely dependent on the motivation and innovation of individuals, groups or divisions rather than from any corporate or departmental lead.  The impact of *Best Value* will encourage greater awareness of customer care and should lead to further improvements.

1.2    The message is clear.  We need, corporately and departmentally, to address promptly and positively the issues of:
- planning a structured approach
- consultation
- communication skills
- publicity
- internal benchmarking
- reviews.

1.3    The department has made a positive start on which to build for the future.  Recommendations for the next steps are given in section 4.

## 2    Introduction

2.1    This report provides an updated summary of the activities and achievements of the department in carrying out the agreed principles of the council's corporate customer care policy.  It looks at where we are now and where we need to be (bearing in mind the requirements of Best Value).  It finally suggests the next steps we need to take to achieve a more assured and focused approach to customer care.

2.2    In 1996 the council approved its six principles of customer care.
       These were to:

       - publish a complaints procedure
       - set and publish standards for the service
       - actively seek the views of customers and staff
       - provide services that are fair and accessible to all
       - explain our services and keep you informed of what is
         happening
       - review our services regularly

       These were reviewed by the Chief Executive in November 1997.
       As part of the department's review, the Director of Social Services
       wrote to each head of division in July 1998 asking for updates on
       progress on each of the six principles.  This report draws on
       information received from each department:

       - *Services for older people*
       - *Children's services*
       - *Planning, Resources & Quality*
       - *Health & Disabilities*

       This report does not take into account developments or progress
       achieved since July 1998.

2.3    Some of the Council's agreed principles of customer care are clearly
       linked to the principles of Best Value - as the table below shows.

| Customer Care Principle | Best Value Principle |
|---|---|
| *Seek views of customers and staff;* *publish complaints procedure* | *Consult and listen to local community* |
| *Review our services regularly* | *Monitor and review services* |
| *Set and publish standards* | *Set targets* |
| *Explain our services and keep people informed* | *Report progress* |

2.4    It is clear to see that the principles of customer care have been an
       excellent grounding for Best Value.

### 3 Where we are: an update on the six principles

**Principle 1:** *publish a complaints procedure*

3.1 As Members will be aware, the department has its own statutory complaints procedure. This has been in place since April 1991. Members receive annual reports on the department's procedure. The Council's corporate complaints procedure, however, was launched in April 1994, and was based on the social services procedure. The general feedback suggests that both procedures are well established and running fairly well. There are a number of good practice examples.

3.2 However, the effectiveness of the social services procedure may well be limited by lack of clear and published standards, poor resourcing, unfocused monitoring that fails to pick up trends or inform planning processes, and variable written communication. The final concern listed points to the need for a departmental (if not corporate) approach to plain English. It is clear that good communication skills are essential to providing effective customer care. It must be realised that writing is a skill; and writing in plain English is a specialised skill. We should consider adopting an approach to plain English as policy, produce staff guidelines, train staff, and monitor outcomes.

| Good Practice | *Day centres for adults with learning disabilities* |
|---|---|
| | Centres have taken the department's procedure and customised it for their service. They have also produced user-friendly publicity aimed at clients - for example, leaflets with pictures, and audio cassette recordings (using the voices of clients themselves). |

| Good Practice | *Planning, Resources &Quality* |
|---|---|
| | The division took positive action to improve the department's procedure and held an independent review. This included talking to people who had gone through the procedure to learn from user experience. A full time designated complaints officer post has now been agreed. |

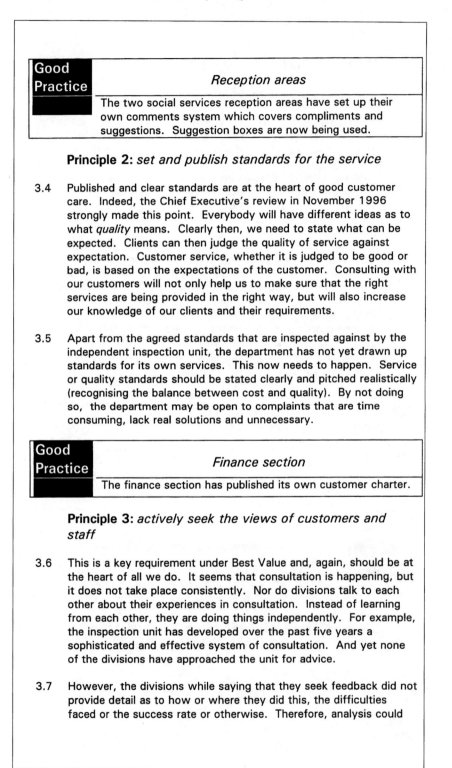

| Good Practice | *Reception areas* |
|---|---|
| | The two social services reception areas have set up their own comments system which covers compliments and suggestions. Suggestion boxes are now being used. |

**Principle 2:** *set and publish standards for the service*

3.4　Published and clear standards are at the heart of good customer care. Indeed, the Chief Executive's review in November 1996 strongly made this point. Everybody will have different ideas as to what *quality* means. Clearly then, we need to state what can be expected. Clients can then judge the quality of service against expectation. Customer service, whether it is judged to be good or bad, is based on the expectations of the customer. Consulting with our customers will not only help us to make sure that the right services are being provided in the right way, but will also increase our knowledge of our clients and their requirements.

3.5　Apart from the agreed standards that are inspected against by the independent inspection unit, the department has not yet drawn up standards for its own services. This now needs to happen. Service or quality standards should be stated clearly and pitched realistically (recognising the balance between cost and quality). By not doing so, the department may be open to complaints that are time consuming, lack real solutions and unnecessary.

| Good Practice | *Finance section* |
|---|---|
| | The finance section has published its own customer charter. |

**Principle 3:** *actively seek the views of customers and staff*

3.6　This is a key requirement under Best Value and, again, should be at the heart of all we do. It seems that consultation is happening, but it does not take place consistently. Nor do divisions talk to each other about their experiences in consultation. Instead of learning from each other, they are doing things independently. For example, the inspection unit has developed over the past five years a sophisticated and effective system of consultation. And yet none of the divisions have approached the unit for advice.

3.7　However, the divisions while saying that they seek feedback did not provide detail as to how or where they did this, the difficulties faced or the success rate or otherwise. Therefore, analysis could not take place to judge the effectiveness of consultation or the ways chosen to carry it out.

3.7     This important part of customer care helps us to understand better the needs of our clients.  We should not only target those who use our services but also those who do not.  For example, we are aware that there is a low uptake of services from ethnic minorities. Successful consultation with these groups will help understand why this is the case, and what we need to do next.

3.9     It is important to remember that staff are also our customers.  For example, the finance section and personnel provide services directly to staff.  Also, in reality managers are the customers of staff, and staff are the customers of managers.  We all rely on others doing their jobs well.  So the quality of communication, systems, procedures and personal support are important ingredients in the customer care mix.  These are all maintained and improved by consulting with and listening to staff.  We should not underestimate this aspect.

| Good Practice | *Inspection Unit* |
|---|---|
| | The Inspection Unit held a seminar (attended by 88 people) to find out what service providers thought about the purpose, principles and methods of inspection. The outcome of the seminar informed a policy document *An Inspector Calls* that sets clear standards for providers to judge the service provided by our inspection unit. |

| Good Practice | *Training section* |
|---|---|
| | A staff suggestion scheme is now in operation. |

**Principle 4**: *provide services that are fair and accessible to all*

3.10   All divisions largely concentrated their comments on this principle to the physical accessibility of buildings.  There seems to be a good awareness of this issue and a number of initiatives are underway. The department has also recently introduced a minicom system, and staff have access to Language Line.

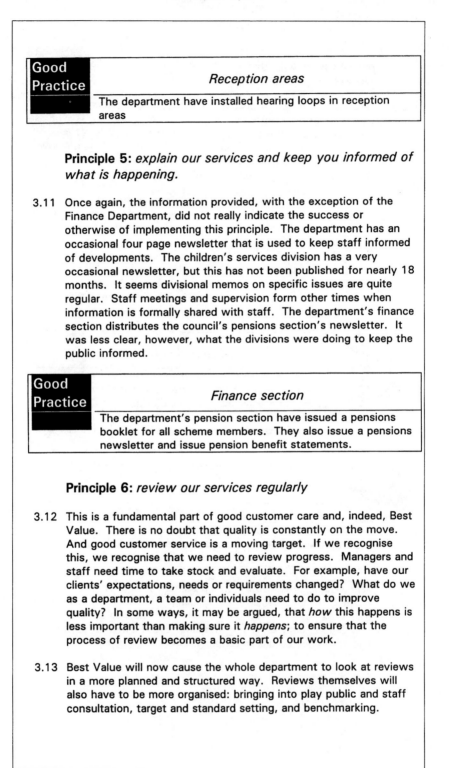

| Good Practice | *Reception areas* |
|---|---|
| | The department have installed hearing loops in reception areas |

### Principle 5: *explain our services and keep you informed of what is happening.*

3.11   Once again, the information provided, with the exception of the Finance Department, did not really indicate the success or otherwise of implementing this principle.  The department has an occasional four page newsletter that is used to keep staff informed of developments.  The children's services division has a very occasional newsletter, but this has not been published for nearly 18 months.  It seems divisional memos on specific issues are quite regular.  Staff meetings and supervision form other times when information is formally shared with staff.  The department's finance section distributes the council's pensions section's newsletter.  It was less clear, however, what the divisions were doing to keep the public informed.

| Good Practice | *Finance section* |
|---|---|
| | The department's pension section have issued a pensions booklet for all scheme members.  They also issue a pensions newsletter and issue pension benefit statements. |

### Principle 6: *review our services regularly*

3.12   This is a fundamental part of good customer care and, indeed, Best Value.  There is no doubt that quality is constantly on the move.  And good customer service is a moving target.  If we recognise this, we recognise that we need to review progress.  Managers and staff need time to take stock and evaluate.  For example, have our clients' expectations, needs or requirements changed?  What do we as a department, a team or individuals need to do to improve quality?  In some ways, it may be argued, that *how* this happens is less important than making sure it *happens*; to ensure that the process of review becomes a basic part of our work.

3.13   Best Value will now cause the whole department to look at reviews in a more planned and structured way.  Reviews themselves will also have to be more organised: bringing into play public and staff consultation, target and standard setting, and benchmarking.

Information received showed that reviews have taken place (for example, the department's complaints procedure) but, in general, reviews have not happened in any consistent, planned or systematic way. Clearly this has to change and, through Best Value, we are now as a department gearing up to meet this challenge.

## 4    The next steps

4.1    A theme of this report has been the potential and actual impact of Best Value on customer care. Best Value will help develop our thinking and commitment to a number of the Council's customer care principles. However, it does seem that we have a lot of ground to make up before we can be confident that customer care is at the heart of our work.

4.2    There needs to be a stronger corporate and departmental focus on customer care, but one that is flexible enough to meet the specialised make up of each division. The recommended next steps follow.

- **Step 1**
  The department's management team should revisit the council's six principles of customer care to re-affirm its commitment.

- **Step 2**
  Once these principles have been re-affirmed or reviewed, each division should go away and agree what these principles mean for their services; then draw up indicators of how they will measure the effectiveness of their performance against these principles. Staff should then be consulted on the indicators.

- **Step 3**
  Once each department has drawn up their customer care charter (or whatever it is agreed to call the document), clients should then be consulted, as appropriate.

- **Step 4**
  Once finally agreed, the customer care principles should be widely publicised both inside and outside the council. The council's free magazine *City Wide* could be used for this (and indeed the public consultation).

- **Step 5**
  If we improve something we should let people know. *City Wide* again could prove useful.  For staff, we could set up a customer care newsletter (which could be council-wide) that highlights innovation and ideas.  This could be a useful first step towards benchmarking within the council for customer care.

- **Step 6**
  We should plan regular and systematic reviews.  These should measure performance against agreed standards and indicators.  The ways of doing this could include customer surveys, sampling techniques, bar-coding letters, 'mystery shoppers' and so on.  Each department and the council as a whole will need to think carefully about this.  Performance should be reported and published.  This will give each department the encouragement to take customer care seriously (as 'what gets measured gets done').  But also it will encourage an approach to monitoring that is efficient in time and cost, but effective on service, morale and client satisfaction.

**David Burrows**                                   **14 September 1998**

# Sources

Alexander, Fran (ed.), *Bloomsbury Thesaurus* (London 1997)
Amis, Kingsley, *The King's English* (London 1997)
Ammer, Christine, *Dictionary of Clichés,* (London 1992)
Andrews, Robert, *Cassell Dictionary of Contemporary Quotations* (London 1996)
Augarde, Tony (ed.), *The Oxford Dictionary of Modern Quotations* (Oxford 1991)
Breen, Peter, *The Book of Letters* (London 1993)
Bryson, Bill, *Troublesome Words* (London 1987)
Burchfield, RW, (ed*)*, *The New Fowler's Modern English Usage* (Oxford 1996)
Burnard, Philip, *Writing for Health Professionals* (London 1996)
Chambers *Combined Dictionary Thesaurus* (Edinburgh 1995)
Chambers *Dictionary of Foreign Words and Phrases* (Edinburgh 1995)
Cohen, JM and MJ, *A Dictionary of Modern Quotations* (London 1973)
Collins *Paperback Dictionary* (New Edition)(London 1995)
Collins *Plain English Dictionary* (London 1996)
*Complete Letter Writer for Gentlemen* (London 1961)
Crystal, David *The English Language* (London 1988)
Crystal, David, *The Cambridge Encyclopedia of Language* (Cambridge 1992)
Doyle, Margaret, *The A-Z of Non-Sexist Language* (London 1995)
Dunant, Sarah (ed.), *The War of the Words* (London 1995)
Fiske, R H, Dictionary of Concise Writing (Cincinnati 1996)
Fowler, H W and Fowler, F G *The King's English (Third Edition)* (Oxford 1996)
Gowers, Ernest, *ABC of Plain Words* (London 1951)
Gowers, Ernest, *Plain Words* (London 1948)
Gowers, Ernest, The *Complete Plain Words* (London 1954)
Howard, Godfrey, *The Good English Guide* (London 1993)
Hyman, R (ed.), *A Dictionary of Famous Quotations* (London 1983)
Kemp, P (ed.), *The Oxford Dictionary of Literary Quotations* (Oxford 1997)
*MacMillan Dictionary of American Slang* (London 1995)
*MacMillan Dictionary of Current English Usage* (London 1995)
Manser, Martin H (ed.), *Good Word Guide (Third Edition)* (London 1997)
Marshall, Jeremy and McDonald, Fred, *Questions of English* (Oxford 1994)
McArthur, Tom, (ed.), *Oxford Companion to the English Language* (Oxford 1992)
Miller, C and Swift K, *The Handbook of Non-Sexist Writing* (London 1995)
Mills, Jane, *Womanwords* (London 1991)
*Oxford Dictionary of English Etymology* (Oxford 1993)
*Oxford Dictionary of English Grammar* (Oxford 1994)
Oxford *Dictionary of Quotations* (Oxford 1990)
*Oxford English* (Oxford 1986)
*Oxford Guide to English Usage* (Oxford 1994)
Partridge, Eric, *Usage and Abusage* (London 1981)
Phythian, B A *Teach Yourself Correct English* (London 1985)
Rees, Nigel, *Letter Writing* (London 1994)
Roget's *Thesaurus* (London 1981)
Schwartz, Marilyn, *Guidelines for Bias-free Writing* (Indiana 1995)
Seely, John, *The Oxford Guide to Writing and Speaking* (Oxford 1998)
*Shorter Oxford English Dictionary* (Oxford 1983)
Strunk, W and White, E B, *The Elements of Style (Third Edition)* (New York 1979)
Summers, Vivian, *Clear English* (London 1991)
Thomson, K Graham, *The Handbook of Letter Writing* (London 1961)
Turner, M D and Abrahamson, R L, *Business Writing* (London 1993)
Van Emden, J & Easteal, J, *Report Writing* (London 1993)

# Index